love yo

IN MY MIND'S EYE

JAN MORRIS

IN MY MIND'S EYE

A Thought Diary

FABER & FABER

First published in 2018
by Faber & Faber Limited
Bloomsbury House, 74–77 Great Russell Street
London WC1B 3DA

Designed by Faber
Printed and bound by CPI Group (UK) Ltd, Croydon, CR0 4YY

The right of Jan Morris to be identified as author of this work
has been asserted in accordance with Section 77 of the Copyright,
Designs and Patents Act 1988

A CIP record for this book
is available from the British Library

ISBN 978-0-571-34091-0

FSC
www.fsc.org
MIX
Paper from
responsible sources
FSC® C020471

2 4 6 8 10 9 7 5 3 1

For
One and All
Kindlily
(and yes, there is such a word!)

DAY I

I have never before in my life kept a diary of my thoughts, and here at the start of my tenth decade, having for the moment nothing much else to write, I am having a go at it. Good luck to me. The first thought that strikes me as being worth memorializing entered my mind today as I drove my dear old Honda Civic Type R (an old friend) into Porthmadog, and on the radio somebody was playing a piano concerto. I sort of knew the tune, but only just, and perhaps what I was remembering came from some other composition altogether? Then it occurred to me how amazing it is that there are still enough unused groupings of musical notes for people to write yet more piano concertos! Won't they ever run out?

And isn't it amazing that there are still all-too-familiar combinations of notes or harmonies, ones I know all too well, that can still bring the tears to my eyes, especially when I am alone driving my car? Nobody to break the spell, I suppose, and perhaps, since my first concentration is upon the driving, the music slides in unaware, like another old friend reminding me of half-forgotten emotions.

DAY 2

In our anguished world of the twenty-first century, when the United States of America I have long cherished is subsumed like everywhere else in squalor and disillusion, I often look back nostalgically to the America I first knew – essentially, in my memory, small-town America. I got to know scores of little towns then, scattered across the entire subcontinent. I had a home for a time in one of them, and I grew to think of them generically as examples of everything I most admired about the great republic.

They were invariably welcoming, almost invariably frank, simple in their loyalties and, well, very nice! Yes, they were very nice places, I used to think, in a very nice country, and jejune though that sounds now, with better adjectives at my command, I remember their essential niceness still.

In those days, of course, sixty or seventy years ago, the mystique of the American small town was more fashionable. Thornton Wilder had made it so, with his play *Our Town*, and popular songs often serenaded it. Like me, they preferred to ignore unhappier truths about Main Street – its likely racism, its probable greed and possible petty corruption – and remembered only its provincial virtues. I am older and more cynical now, but I still prefer to remember those old stereotypes, with the housewives nattering and the volunteers swapping tall tales at the fire station, and the friendly handful of black people, and the swanky young bloods showing off when the town pond froze at Christmas.

With those fond, if fanciful, memories, too, went a related patriotism, bold but genial, to which I happily subscribed. As a national heritage I am devoted to my own British past, because I like the colour and eccentricity of it, the effrontery, the mixture of greed and benevolence, the admirable, the unforgivable, the bombast and the humour – all of which is still best expressed, I think, by the ambiguous epic of the late British Empire, to which I have devoted much of my life.

But the Pax Britannica was, of course, famously nationalistic, and when it comes to a profounder kind of patriotism, it strikes me that the old American sort was far grander and truer, based as it was not upon triumphs, but upon the original generous values of the republic. If I were to choose a new national anthem for the USA, I would choose the words by Emma Lazarus that are inscribed upon the plinth of the Statue of Liberty. They welcome the world's masses, tired, hungry and oppressed, through the Golden Gates to freedom, and I would sing them to the setting written in 1949 by a refugee from Russian Siberia.

And I would have it sung, if possible, by the Mormon Tabernacle Choir of Salt Lake City, who originally modelled themselves – wait for it – upon the male voice choirs of my own dear Wales.

DAY 3

Conscience doth make cowards of us all, the man said, but my conscience simply makes me ashamed of myself, and is often not quite powerful enough to curb my inner devil. A person I very much dislike lives quite near me, and when I drove home in today's heavy rainstorm I noticed that four or five items of her washing were flapping on her line in the rain. She is away on holiday, and Conscience prodded me. Shouldn't I stop and take the things in out of the wet? Nobody else will.

'So what?' said my personal Beelzebub. 'There's nothing on that line but a few old socks, dusters and stuff. Why should she care if they got wet?'

Conscience disagreed. 'They may not look much to you,' it said, 'but perhaps they are precious to her.'

Beelzebub: 'More fool her for leaving them there.'

Conscience: 'I thought your life's motto was "Be Kind"?'

Beelzebub: 'Believe me, if it was your things that were getting wet, she most certainly wouldn't bother about them.'

Conscience: 'Well, I'm not her, am I?'

Beelzebub: 'No, thank goodness, you don't go around being goody-goody and thinking you're better than anyone else. Besides, you know very well that she is a person you very much dislike. Remember?'

'By God, you're right,' I told him, and hurried straight home out of the rain.

DAY 4

In the middle of the night I awoke with the need to have a shit (a marvellously expressive word, you must agree, and first recorded in English, so my *OED* tells me, in 1308; Tom Wolfe once recorded thirty-two distinct usages of it).

This was a new annoyance for me, and leads me to record now all the symptoms of senility, or worse, that afflict me in my tenth decade: (1) loss of physical balance; (2) forgetfulness; (3) excessive urination; (4) a sort of freezing sensation in my toes at night; (5) more or less permanent catarrh; (6) miscellanious pains in my abdomen, back, spine, heart region and stomach; (7) inability to spell perfectly familiar words like 'miscellaneous'; (8) bubbles in my ears; (9) irritability; (10) envy; (11) fading pleasures of wine (I used to claim that I had drunk a glass of wine every day since the Second World War; now I sometimes go a week without one!); (12) embarrassing forgetfulness of names, faces or acquaintanceships (is there such a word?); (13) excessive literary reliance upon the exclamation mark.

And now, to cap it all, the nocturnal need to defecate. But, anyway, it all adds up to that most maddening of all afflictions: old age, or senility. To my mind the Bible was sensible to suggest seventy as a proper span of human life. John Donne was perhaps a little pessimistic to suggest that we 'love nobly, and live, till we arrive to write three-score', but Shakespeare was dead right, as always, to warn us that our seventh age would be unquestionably the worst of them all.

'What's your recipe for a happy old age?' somebody asked me the other day, rashly assuming that I was enjoying one, and I could only answer enigmatically, as I always do, 'Be kind!'

DAY 5

Some novels, I fear, are just too clever for me or, rather, I am not clever enough for them. Sometimes, though, it seems to me that they are just too clever for their own good. Of course, I relish the challenge of a superior artistic intellect, even if I need help to understand it. For eighteen years I failed to get through Joyce's *Ulysses*, until I was delightfully converted to its genius by Harry Blamires's key to it all, and since then I have never looked back. I am still of the impertinent opinion, though, that such a great masterpiece would be even greater if it could be scoured of unnecessary obscurities, while its successor, *Finnegans Wake*, since nobody I know has ever succeeded in reading it all the way through, seems to me a perfect waste of the master's time.

All this is because I have now reached, with muddled feelings, page 38 of Gabriel García Márquez's *One Hundred Years of Solitude* (1967). I am reading it, a bit late in the day, because I feel I ought to. The *New York Times*, I see, says it should be required reading for the whole human race. I shall soon know whether all of it is going to be required reading for me.

Later: No.

DAY 6

Am I superstitious? I suppose I am. Agnosticism is a long way from atheism, and I honour some old folk-beliefs, fads and taboos partly out of habit and partly – well, why not? Touching wood, throwing salt, walking under ladders, using the number thirteen are all things I prefer to do or not to do, according to ancient pagan or religious references, and one might as well honour them, don't you think?

Talking to things is a rather different sort of illogicality, though, and here I offer no excuse. No Druidical seer has obliged me to talk aloud to my books or thank a good omelette. There is no immemorial precedent, so far as I know, for my morning conversations with my toothbrush or my night-time expressions of gratitude to the furniture. The TV doesn't in the least care whether I enjoy its programmes, and that constantly dripping tap clearly doesn't listen to me anyway. There is no logic, I well know, to the habit of talking to inanimate objects, and I do it only, I suppose, because it gives me some sense of fellowship or camaraderie.

If you are a believer, of course, talking to your chosen omnipotent deity is a different matter, and lifelong incredulist that I am, in the terrible times we inhabit, with new horrors erupting every day across the world, I do sometimes offer a sympathetic message to whatever almighty power there may or may not be out there.

'Goodnight, God!' I say, as I turn my bedside light off (if the wretched thing works, that is). 'Goodnight, and good luck to you!'

DAY 7

On a gloomy afternoon I pluck from my discs a collection of songs with words and music by Irving Berlin, and the first phrase that I hear is something very sentimental to do with the moon. I would quote it for you were it not for astronomic copyright charges.

Dear God, I ask myself, is that really the sort of thing you like? Well, I admit to a particular bias. Irving Berlin was the very first American I ever met, and when I was invited to take part in the BBC radio programme *Desert Island Discs*, every one of my chosen records was by him. But forget the moon bit. I admire Berlin for his lyrical genius, his grand, simple tunes and his universal appeal, and this is also what I admire most in the music of the grandest classical composers of them all.

It is, I know, a populist preference, the love of tunes and melody, but I am prepared to bet that from Bach to Mahler, Mozart to Wagner to Prokofiev, the masters would forgive me and share my admiration for the Jerome Kerns and Richard Rodgerses of our own centuries. Would Chopin have appreciated 'All the Things You Are'? Of course he would, and would probably have hummed it to George Sand in the Majorcan twilight. 'I've written a marvellous tune!' exulted Edward Elgar (he of the Cello Concerto): it was 'Land of Hope and Glory'. He who made the Lamb made the Tyger, too!

Heaven knows I am not alone, anyway. How many of us have not found our attention wandering as we await the next delicious aria at the opera, or our patience challenged as we sit through some interminable medieval anthem, dying for the final festivity of a Victorian hymn? But mind you, it is true that a Berlin melody feels rather less ethereal when it is not sung by Fred Astaire – subliminally dancing to it as he sings, so to speak. Only the very greatest of all the tunes, I suspect, do not depend upon their interpretations, even in our own minds, but like the greatest of poems are always hovering out there in the ether, whether we are paying attention or not.

DAY 8

On the subject of talking to things, talking to animals is, of course, another matter. We all talk to our dogs, cats and horses, do we not, and assume that they have at least a glimmer of understanding in response. The dog smiles, in a way. Addicts assure me that the horse (not one of my favourites) shows genuine gratitude for its fodder. And the cat undoubtedly purrs.

Ay, and there's the rub. Your cat purrs when it is comfortable, but it also purrs to show extreme hostility. Perhaps it purrs when it is all alone? Perhaps its purr means nothing really, and is in no way intended to please you? Cat-lovers will excoriate me for expressing such heresies, and dear old ladies, fondling their dear pussies, will send me angry letters of reprimand.

They need not bother, though, for of course my own cat, Ibsen, is an exception to the rule – or was, for he died some time ago, and I shall never have another. Naturally, he was grateful to me. Naturally, he purred to express his friendship. Naturally, he was true. He was a Norwegian Forest cat, which is why he was named Ibsen, and so sure am I of his integrity, and of our mutual understanding down the years, that I think of him as an equal. All other cats may just be cats, but my cat Ibsen was a friend and a colleague.

My cat Ibsen was different . . . like all the rest of them. Ask your Aunt Agatha.

DAY 9

Is there such a person as an incredulist, which I claimed myself to be the other day? Of course there is. It is a person who is by nature or practice an unbeliever in the first instance, and suspects that on the whole, all being equal, notwithstanding, nevertheless, most of life is more likely to be false than true – when all is said and done, that is, and all things considered. It seems to me that the existence of such a person is self-evident (I am one myself, am I not?), yet the *Oxford English Dictionary* does not recognize the word. I can be an incredule, it seems, or at least I could have been in 1590, when a fierce hymnist cried, 'Increduils hence ga hide you hie!', but never so far an incredulist.

Not until now! Here and now I offer contemporary English a new word, and declare my admiration for an entity that has, down the centuries, so generously absorbed additions, changes and new inflexions into its ancient and ever flexible self. All the same, I wish youngish English or anglicized persons, if I ask them how they are, would not now say 'Good, thank you,' as Americans do. I am not inquiring about their moral condition, only their state of health.

DAY 10

In the street today I almost bumped into a sort of miniature woman – not a very small one, not a dwarf, but a four-year-old, perhaps, with all the attributes of a grown-up. She wore spectacles, which helped the illusion, and a sweetly floral summer frock and sandals, and she moved politely out of my way to let me pass. But here's the creepy thing: her smile was altogether the smile of an adult – which is to say, it was switched on and switched off almost automatically, the very abrogation of innocence. I have sometimes noticed this among children in China, but never before in Wales.

Years ago, early in a wandering life, I devised something called the Smile Test, by which to measure something of the character of a city and its people. It involved smiling resolutely at strangers I met in the street and analysing their responses. Long ago, for instance, I determined that the responses of passing pedestrians in Vancouver accurately assessed that city's innate characteristics of exceptional decency but inhibiting uncertainty. Generalizations are dangerous and impertinent, I know, but there we are, it was my trade.

Now that my travelling days are limited and I more seldom leave Wales, I more often employ the Smile Test to explore the national characteristics of that puzzling ethnic community, the English. I am half English myself, and have devoted much of my career to commemorating the historical exploits of what we used to call Britain and is now tentatively known as the United Kingdom, but I am prouder of my Welsh 50 per cent, and having lived in Wales for more than seventy years, long ago came to regard the myriad English tourists from over our border as more or less foreigners.

And what does the test tell me of them? That there is now no such thing as an English character. So powerful and unmistakeable used it to be that one could tell an Englishman, as they used to say, a mile (1,609.34 metres) away, but it was a people's character moulded by a long triumphant history, by a functional class system, by the instincts of imperialism and by generations of national confidence. Peer or pauper, man or woman, Eton or comprehensive, English people were proud of being English and used to being respected.

Try the Smile Test now as a middle-aged, obviously English couple approach us down the promenade. We turn the smile on and wait for a passing response. There is none. Not a flicker of a response. Their eyes are resolutely averted. They look, if not actually scared, at least suspicious. It is as though they never expect the best, only the worst, as though if we are not actually going to harm them, we might be laughing at them. Far from responding *de haut en bas*, as the world used to expect of them, or with the confident fraternity that we might look for today, or even with their once-famous national humour, they look as though they have been reprimanded by destiny. Perhaps they have?

'Cheer up, we're friends!' I always feel like telling them as we pass, but they don't look round, so I go on my way whistling, notwithstanding.

My vicarious friend Alberto Manguel (I have never met him, except by mail) has become director of the National Library of Argentina, in succession to the great Jorge Luis Borges. Borges was blind during his tenure, which must surely have restricted his contemporary reading, but nobody can be more widely read in literature old and new than Manguel, who has not only written books about the very practice of reading, but possesses a magnificent private library of his own.

I cannot help wondering, though, if he can ever feel the same about the millions of books now in his care at the Biblioteca Nacional and the thousands that belong to him at home. For myself, I have rarely used books in public libraries, extravagantly preferring always to buy my own, and this means that my relationship with them is genuinely emotional, even, at a pinch, physical. 'Ah, your very best friends are here, I see,' said a perceptive old Welsh guest of ours, passing among my own bookshelves at the end of a dinner party, and he had a point. I dearly love the feel and intimate presence of my books, the look of them, the smell of them and, above all, their lingering associations (there is hardly a volume in my collection that does not have a memory attached to it, if not in an actual letter, postcard or newspaper cutting, then at least in a blurred emotion). Now that I am ancient, pottering among such old acquaintances is one of my redemptive pleasures.

Surely dear Alberto's pride and loyalty must be torn between the vast impersonal stock of associates that are his public responsibility and all those myriad friends awaiting him after supper at home? But no, he is wiser than I am, and cleverer, and he knows it is the Word that counts.

DAY 13

My car having gone in for servicing, I have been lent a very elaborate Renault, and fiddling about with its innumerable switches, wondering how the petrol goes in or the windows open, confused by its various bleeps and flashing warnings, it has occurred to me how quickly technology becomes old-fashioned, and how ungainly it soon seems to one of my temperament.

There are many people I know, all over the world, who are enthralled by the lost magic of steam, but what a messy sort of djinn that was! The dirt of it! The noise! The smoke! How miserable, the spectacle of those grimy firemen forever shovelling coal into the fireboxes! Even the gleam of brass failed to give beauty to the hulking great shapes of the steam locomotives, and to my mind there was something really rather comical about the spectacle of all those trucks and carriages trundling one after the other across a landscape behind a puffing engine, forlornly hooting sometimes – and occasionally, I have learnt from picture books of my childhood, sticking a kind of net out to catch mail bags waiting for it on the side of the track!

And not much less laughable, it seems to me, is my Renault, so determined to be modern, so cluttered with switches and symbols, things to press and warning lights to look out for. But never mind, I tell myself, the internal combustion engine will soon be as obsolete as those dirty old steam mechanisms, and the next generation's cars, already just around the corner, will all be electric – elegant, quiet, cool and clean.

Unless, of course, they are nuclear, and even then their detritus merely has to be buried for a couple of centuries to lose its evil potency.

DAY 14

Ah, what the sun can do! I sat in a seaside café this morning, a morning of sunshine at last, and watched the holiday crowds swarm by outside. Yesterday, after long hours of rain and cloud, they looked, en masse, not just unhealthily fat, but corporately morose. It was as though they had brought with them, from some despondent homeland, an inherited lack of hope. Even the children looked bored. Their parents seemed to be counting the hours till the train home, while the occasional grandmothers were mostly dressed as if for some sort of neighbourhood protest concerning unsafe traffic crossings, perhaps, or waste collections.

But look at them now, now that the sun shines! One and all, they are transformed! They laugh merrily back at me through my café window! Those grannies are not in greens and greys now, but dazzling in primary colours, while the mums and dads seem miraculously to have lost weight, in their sudden baseball caps, shorts, sandals and winsomely provocative cottons. As for the children, boys and girls, all of whom now seem to be more or less five years old, they are uniformly enchanting and bursting with health, as though they have spent all their lives in fairyland!

Could it be so? Of course not, bless their hearts. The change is only in me, all curmudgeonly prejudice banished by the genial sun and seeing, over my cappuccino, only the best in the morning world.

DAY 15

Is this the start of Alzheimer's? I had a sleepless night last night, but as I turned this way and that, switched the radio on and off, tried my best to clear my mind into emptiness, I knew perfectly well just what it was that was keeping me awake. It was –

Well, what was it? There's the rub. Today the cause of my insomnia has gone clean out of my mind. Absolutely evident last night, utterly blank this morning. Is this a first inkling of that wretched condition we all read about, or is it simply what we used to call Old Age? Long ago the writer Elspeth Huxley, who spent some of her later years near us in Wales, told me that a queer thing had happened to her: now and then she simply could not recall perfectly ordinary English words and had to look them up in a thesaurus. She died in 1997, but now I wonder how she later got on with the spelling of them. I find myself that sometimes the spelling of some absolutely familiar and ordinary word gets so muddled in my mind that, like Elspeth with her thesaurus, I am obliged to reach for my *Shorter Oxford* . . .

One of my oldest friends in life, one of the kindest and cleverest, was faced in his last decade by a far more terrible challenge. He was as quick and kindly as ever, but his beloved loving wife of many years suddenly and inexplicably declined to recognize him – not only that, but she also took a violent dislike to him. That was more than old age, wasn't it? That was the inexplicable evil of Alzheimer's at its worst, and if I were not an agnostic it would make me seriously doubt the existence of a merciful God.

In the meantime . . .

I have always rather envied the poet Ovid, who was banished from Rome by the Emperor Augustus, you may remember, to a remote place called Tomis on the shores of the Black Sea. There he died, ten years later, and his exile has gone into legend and into art – Turner's commemoration of his fate is as poignantly dramatic as *The Fighting Temeraire*. Ovid wrote prodigiously during his banishment, and although his work was mostly sad and often complaining, as a remote member of the same fraternity I find it hard to commiserate with him. There are worse predicaments, it seems to me, than enforced residence in a house on the Black Sea writing lyric poetry for the rest of your life.

Tomis is now the hefty Romanian port of Constanța, not a bad sort of place at all, with a big nineteenth-century statue of Ovid in a square named for him, but my own Tomis is our garden yard at Llanystumdwy, Wales. It is Elizabeth's domain: she created it and attends it still. I just laze about in it thinking up compositions, Ovid-like. It is a patch of gravel overlooked on three sides by a tangled mass of trees and bushes: a fir or two, a horse chestnut, rhododendrons, bushes of camellia interspersed with blackberry brambles, shrubs I don't know the names of, primroses, bluebells and snowdrops when the season allows, miscellaneous weeds here and there that Elizabeth heroically resists. The whole ensemble is presided over by a splendid old sycamore, dominating the skyline.

I must not make it sound too grand. There is nothing grand about it. It is essentially homely, and its fascination for me is that it is not just home for us, but for a myriad of other creatures! Half a century ago I bought a wonderful book, *The Living House* by George Ordish, which told me that at that time his house probably accommodated two hundred residential spiders, besides miscellaneous colonies of beetles, fleas, moths, cockroaches and flies. I love to think about the livestock similarly living, eating, fighting, procreating and dying in and around the yard all around me, as I laze there in the sunshine and Elizabeth deals with weeds.

Not long ago there was certainly more of it, but the shifting ecology has robbed us of the grass snakes, glow-worms and occasional lizards that used to frequent the place – even the toads seem scarcer. Never mind, butterflies visit me as I laze, bees and wasps buzz around, beetles and caterpillars make for the gravel, sometimes a handsome dragonfly comes up from the river or a robin hops in. A sudden scuffle in the bushes means that a clumsy squirrel or two are in there – and yes, there they are leaping erratically from branch to branch. More often a crow or a blackbird swoops or cackles among the trees, and a wood pigeon monotonously serenades its mate. Sometimes coveys of seagulls from Cardigan Bay pass overhead, on their way to a promising harvesting somewhere. Our owls are still asleep, I suppose, but I like to think of them anyway, there in the dark of the woods.

25

Ah, but here comes our merry postman, with his morning consignment of trash. Elizabeth drops her trowel and pops off to make some coffee, and I pull myself together, stretch, send my respectful regards to Ovid and the emperor, and leave the yard to the rest of them.

DAY 17

On the matter of melody. One of my less disturbing troubles is the well-known affliction of tunes in one's head. It is not much of an affliction in my own case because I never have tunes in there which I do not like, but sometimes even the best of them stick up there too long, like tetanus, and can be debilitating, occupying hour after hour a sizeable chunk of my brain. What is it about melodies? How is it that a simple arrangement of sounds can affect us so, to tears or laughter or obsession?

I endured such a tetanal malady recently (yes, there is such an adjective), and it was doubly obsessive because for the life of me I couldn't remember what the tune was. I was sure it was something enormously famous and familiar, but what in God's name was it? Showbiz or classic, First World War or the Beatles or . . .? For long days, perpetually hearing it in my mind, I demanded of other people if they knew it – not just friends, but even strangers I bumped into at the supermarket, to any of whom I burbled a snatch of the melody. Almost all recognized it, but only one man finally knew what it was – a theme not from an old stage show or movie tear-jerker, but from the second movement of Beethoven's piano sonata 'La Pathétique'. You know the one, of course you do!

How I thanked him! I almost hugged him. After all that time the sublime melody left my mind at last, and I

27

replaced it for a month or two with 'One Day When We Were Young' (music by Johann Strauss II, 1885; words by Oscar Hammerstein II, 1938).

DAY 18

I have lately been the subject of a television programme, presided over by one of the best-known and best-loved professionals in the business, and the effect on me has been disastrous.

I have lived in this corner of Wales for seventy years, and my family and I are sufficiently well known. I can't go shopping without bumping into old acquaintances, and one of the delights of Wales anyway is its organic sense of comradeship. Appearing on TV, though, seduced me into altogether different sensations. Suddenly, I felt, all those familiar people treated me in quite a new way. All of a sudden, they seemed to me actually eager to say hullo, as though my appearance on the screen beside that universally admired personality had somehow anointed me with an unction! Many of them had read books of mine, lots had been kind and helpful to me over the decades, but now it was as though they were greeting an altogether new me.

And a new me it was, alas. Not them. Me. Something of the dross of television had rubbed off on me, the tinsel magic of it and the awful distortions of celebrity. I found I was actually offended if somebody didn't mention that TV programme (which I hadn't even seen myself), and actually disturbed if somebody didn't recognize me at all. Dear God, how eagerly I turned to Twitter each morning, in search of favourable comments. Never in a long life of writing books had I hungered so avidly for good reviews!

But it soon wore off. Things got back to normal, and people no longer seemed to prepare their smiles for me as I approached them down the road. The reviews petered out. The programme was forgotten, and its presiding personality moved on to other avenues of fame. In the end, I actually saw the programme myself, and what did I see?

Through the eyes of candour I saw a very old woman in yellow, shuffling.

DAY 19

Was it hallucinatory? Was it real? Am I going off my head? When I came down to breakfast the other morning there scuttled across the library floor a very small jet-black animal, smaller than a mouse, like a mole or a vole, perhaps. It vanished instantly, and I could find no trace of it under any table, bookcase, rug or carpet. Ten minutes later, when I was sitting on a sofa with my coffee, out of the corner of my eye I saw, just for a moment, the suggestion of another little black something down by my feet, and then . . . dear me, yes, for a second or two there was that small black creature again, with an obvious tail now. In a blink of my eye it was gone, somewhere into nowhere, and there has been no sign of it ever since – no scratching, no droppings, only the fleeting glimpses in my mind of that little black scuttling object. Was it real? Did I truly see it? Was it my first hallucination?

Watch this space.

My basic form of daily exercise is this: I walk for a thousand paces up and down the lane beside our house. It amounts to about a mile, and I supplement it, of course, with further exertions, but the thousand paces is my self-imposed basic discipline, rain, shine or earthquake.

It is sometimes a bit of a bore, but I do it at a fairly brisk march, sustained by the discipline of rhythmic breathing and by whistling, singing, humming or just imagining suitably pulsating works of music. My mental repertoire of these is wide, from 'Men of Harlech' to Mozart's 'Dies irae', but yesterday I decided to narrow the scope to national anthems, which would surely keep my marching proud and steady.

Well, off I set, on a fine morning too, and I began at once, of course, with 'Hen Wlad Fy Nhadau' – 'Land of my Fathers' – which got me going at a spanking pace. 'God Save the Queen' came next, to the tune that Beethoven respected, and which also supports the American 'My Country, 'Tis of Thee' and Leichtenstein's 'Oben am jungen Rhein'. And what could be more invigorating than 'La Marseillaise', with the swagger of the Republican Guard? Or 'Scotland the Brave', to the grand swirl of the pipes?

Presently, though, I ran out of national anthems (Italy? Spain? Russia? China?), and somewhere about pace five hundred I fell back upon unofficial substitutes. Now it was

'(I'm a) Yankee Doodle Dandy' and 'Waltzing Matilda' and 'Land of Hope and Glory' and 'When Irish Eyes Are Smiling' and 'Colonel Bogey', but just when things were getting a bit tawdry, another true national anthem crept into my mind and transported me elsewhere for a moment, far from our bumpy lane on this brisk Welsh morning and back to an evening function at the Brandenburg Gate in Berlin, long years ago.

They were officially celebrating the two hundredth birthday of that dread monument, which had seen so many demonstrations of Prussian pomp and Nazi arrogance, and I went to the affair that evening with some distaste; but when it drew to an end and I expected a last brassy evocation of hubris, instead there stole into the dusk Haydn's infinitely gentle arrangement of 'Deutschland, Deutschland über alles', surely the greatest of all national anthems, in the mellow adaptation of a string quartet.

And so I did my final paces this morning, avoiding the puddle by the farm gates, not to a martial discipline, but to a sad and more graceful euphony.

DAY 21

'Stop the world,' cried Anthony Newley's smash musical of 1966, 'I want to get off!', and legend says he took the title from a graffito somewhere. The sentiment was common enough then, when the hydrogen bomb was maturing, and it is probably even more widely held now, when the world seems inextricably entangled in conflicts political, economic and ironically religious, not to mention just plain deranged. I meet plenty of people of my own generation, matured in decades of disillusionment, who suspect today's state of the earth to be its most absolutely frightful ever, and who might very well agree with Mr Newley's graffitist.

I don't, though. I'm prepared to stick it out. It is true that I sometimes feel, as Pope said of the vestal virgins, 'The world forgetting, by the world forgot,' but it's no more than a spasm. I shan't be here much longer anyway, and I would be ashamed to desert my family and friends – after all, the human race may merely be undergoing a temporary period of insanity, as against its usual condition of confusion. Besides, although heaven knows I have enough to worry about in my personal affairs, like nearly everyone else, I have lots to enjoy too, and lots of people to like and love.

So, no, I don't want to desert the old earth. The most desperate graffito you might find on my bedroom wall would only be 'Stop the alarm clock. I don't want to get up.'

Preoccupied as I am during my daily exercise up our
lane, eyes on the ground, thinking about something else
altogether, I seldom know exactly where I am on the route.
Kind nature, though, has provided a key to let me know
when it is time to turn around and walk home again. The
lane runs parallel with the little river Dwyfor, with some
woodlands in between, and unless after a rainfall the
water is running very high, I hear nothing of it for the first
half-mile of my bemused exercise. Then the lane leaves the
woodland and the river grows closer, and for the first time
I am conscious of the rush of its stream. Without a pause,
I turn at once and begin my homeward march.

This frequent little experience reminds me, oddly
enough, of Swaziland, a country not in most respects
much like Wales. There, long years ago, I learnt that high
on a mountainside above Mbabane was a sacred glade in
which the remains of all Swazi kings down the centuries
had been traditionally scattered. How could I get there, I
inquired, and they told me that I must follow a track up
the mountain that itself clung to the course of a stream,
and that – wait for it! – the moment I could no longer hear
the rush of its waters, I would know I was on holy ground.

Was I? I swear I felt, when the water fell silent, some
profound unworldly influence that held me motionless
there; just as, when I hear the Dwyfor near the end of

our lane, I instantly turn for home. There is a difference, though. When I get home from my daily exercise I feel fine, but when I returned from the sanctuary of the Swazi kings that evening, so my notes of the time remind me, I spent the next two days inexplicably sick in bed.

DAY 23

I stumbled yesterday upon a tragedy. High above the sea near our home in Wales is a lonely windswept graveyard, with a small attendant church. The graveyard feels more important than the church, which is locked. It is far away from the nearest houses, but it is well mown and tended and clearly cherished; there are many new gravestones among the rows and rows of slabs and crosses undulating across the surrounding grassland. Pottering idly around it yesterday I recognized many of the family names there from homes and farms and shops near our own house. Some were in English, some in Welsh, and it seemed to me an enviable place to end up, high in those silent meadows above the sea. It was like a community still, tradesmen and seafaring people and shopkeepers and farmers and such – not so different, I thought, from the community we still are in the district all around.

In a remote corner of the cemetery, though, I noticed a sadder kind of memorial. Within its own enclosure was a tall grey obelisk, crumbled a little. Its surrounding turf was unkempt and its inscriptions looked hard to decipher, but it was still a commanding sort of presence, separate from the unassuming ranks around it. I scrambled up there, and found that it commemorated three members of the Ward family, unknown to me and altogether distinct, I felt, from that homely society of the dead.

The obelisk commemorated Brigadier General Thomas Ward, 1861–1949, of the famous British cavalry regiment the Queen's Bays, and his wife Cathleen, 1887–1972, identified as a daughter of the Earl of Belmore. What a world away, I thought, from the rest of their neighbours in their burial place, and how ironically telling their position in that obelisked corner of the graveyard seemed! But then, around the other side, I found a third epitaph, to their son Lieutenant Richard Thomas Ward, Military Cross, 1924–1944, also of the Queen's Bays, and my responses changed.

Consider the dates. The old general was eighty-three, his Cathleen fifty-seven, when their brave boy Richard, in his twentieth year, was killed in action in Italy in the Second World War. Were they really so apart, after all, from the community of the dead in that quiet graveyard in the wind? Was not their sorrow the sorrow of them all – of all of us too, for that matter?

DAY 24

Do you remember India's Grand Trunk Road, as Kipling described it in *Kim* – 'A wonderful spectacle . . . a river of life . . . green-arched, shade-flecked . . . the white breadth speckled with slow-pacing folk'? Well, I saw it for myself this evening, looking along our lane to the farmyard.

It was a jammed little cameo up there, half in shade, framed by the thick green trees of our avenue, and it seemed to be in slow, stately movement along the great highway, somewhere between Allahabad and Amritsar perhaps. There were a dominant couple of elephants, laboriously swaying, and coveys of peasants jostled along the pavements, and I could hear laughter sometimes, and see a pi-dog scurrying mischievously here and there among the dust clouds. High-wheeled wagons were edging their way through the melee; once, a small busy rickshaw darted in and out of the traffic. O I could see all the colours of India along there, and smell its smells, and hear the reedy half-tones of its music magically in the air.

For it was five o'clock, you see. And my neighbours the Parrys were taking their Hereford cows in for milking, riding their quad bikes, with Ben the dog scampering all around. The pace was unhurried. The light flickered with floating oak leaves. The dust was hay dust. It was me

39

really, whistling those arcane melodies, and that bustling rickshaw was only my own Honda, hurrying me home to tea from the supermarket bazaar.

DAY 25

I read somewhere the other day about a man who fell in love with a sheep. It sounded an unsatisfactory affair to me, but not half so unsatisfactory as being a sheep. Was there ever an animal so utterly without romance? I know Christians long ago adopted it as a very model of innocence, favoured by God himself, but living as I do in the heart of sheep country, and coming across the animals almost every day of my life, I find the meek and mildness beloved of the hymnists depressing to a degree.

Not least because when it is a lamb, the sheep really can be truly enchanting in its playfulness, romping joyously around with its fellows, falling off logs, suddenly dashing across the field for another communal suck at the maternal udder. Lamb of God I can well accept. Sheep of God is unimaginable. As far as I can see, the adult sheep does nothing at all but eat. It hardly ever utters that dullest of all animal cries, the baa (a sound which does not even qualify for italics, since I see that today's *Oxford Dictionary*, like Dr Johnson's in 1755, recognizes it as a word). The sheep must procreate, but one never sees it happening. No, it simply stands there among its identical fellows, silent, almost motionless, colourless, just munching, munching, munching, nibbling time away . . . If there were such a thing as transmigration, I would give almost anything not to be reborn as a sheep.

On the other hand, to be a Goat! Wow! A creature born to a capital letter is Capricorn the Goat, clever, capricious, bearded, elegantly horned and hoofed, magically antic. Surely to join his peculiar company must be an ultimate ambition of the afterlife? Besides, I happen to know, by occult intelligence, that the Goat will ultimately accede to the governance of the earth, in alliance with left-handed humans.

DAY 26

I've had enough of capitalism. When I was young and easy, I thought of it, I suppose, in homely terms of biscuit makers, chocolates, Raleigh bicycles, W. H. Smith's bookshops and paternal country bank managers. The business magnates we read about then all seemed to be enlightened employers of evangelist leanings who built model villages for their employees. I had never been to the City of London, and Wall Street meant far less to me than the Golden Road to Samarkand.

In my adolescence, Karl Marx turned up, and I learnt, in broad terms, that capitalists were one and all villains, down to the corner newsagent. Then Hitler arrived with another set of dogmas, and by the time Stalinism had come and gone I was grown up and had reached the conclusion that, on the whole, capitalist democracy was, as Churchill apparently thought, the least bad of them all.

I read with admiration in those days of the great British companies whose presence and influence spanned the whole world – laudable substitutes, I vaguely thought, for the subsiding British Empire. I believed the City of London, in its innumerable facets, to be an honourable expression of British values, and I was genuinely touched when, trying to pay my bill with a dollar cheque on a liner in the Persian Gulf, I was told rather snootily by the purser, 'Oh dear me, no. On the ships of this line we prefer the pound sterling . . .'

43

But look at British capitalism now, the basic economic system of our kingdom! I admit I know almost nothing about it. I have met very few genuine capitalists in my life, and they have all been admirable: one started a highly successful book auctioneering firm, another went in for commercial hydro-gardening, and there are half a dozen small private enterprises here around me in Wales whose style and purposes I much admire. But as a whole, from what I read about the British ruling ideology nowadays, it seems to be just one vulgar scam!

Who are its heroes now? Where is its morality? Any pious Quakers in those boardrooms? Any visionary philanthropists online? The money-making champions of our time all too often seem to be show-off celebrities with glittery wives, vast offshore assets, mansions in Monaco or Jamaica, dubious financial records, shaky sexual reputations, enormous vulgar yachts and an apparently complicit readiness to be pictured in the pages of *Hello!* magazine.

But does the system work? you may say. Does it keep the old kingdom steady as she goes? Would Winston approve? Well, he surmised that the British Empire might last a thousand years, and he was wrong about that . . .

DAY 27

'Anathema' is a good word, don't you think? It rolls well off the tongue, it is rhythmically satisfying and its meaning is ominously indistinct. Anathema! One would hardly wish anathema to one's worst enemy!

Well, I wish it, here and now, to anyone who has anything to do with zoos. They call them zoological gardens nowadays, but they are really prisons – jails for living creatures utterly innocent of crime, imprisoned without trial generally far from home, with no hope of reprieve and no pretence at justice. I accept no excuses from those who run or benefit from these appalling institutions. I realize that most of them believe there is some fundamental difference of privilege between mankind and the rest of the animal kingdom – or, as some would say, that animals can have no souls. Balderdash, I would say to them.

It's no good telling me that zoos are necessary for the survival of endangered species. That's like claiming that when the Tasmanian aboriginal people faced extinction, the last of them should have been locked up for preservation purposes. To my mind all the scientific research in the world cannot make up for the imprisonment of a single creature in a zoo. If vivisection is required, use human volunteers. If there aren't any, tough.

Nor do I excuse from my contempt people who go to zoos for pleasure, particularly those who take their children

45

along and encourage them, licking their ice creams, to stare through the bars, over the ditches or through the prison glass at their helpless fellow creatures inside. If anything, I despise them most of all, especially when they claim that it offers their offspring 'an educational experience'.

For them I reserve full anathema, for it can be much more than a wish or a simple expression of dislike. Since ancient times it has been a powerful, full-blown curse, and I cast it now, with capital As and exclamation marks, on all zoos everywhere, all zoos there have ever been, and all people since the beginning of time (children excepted, of course) who have used any of these despicable places for profit or for pleasure.

ANATHEMA upon them! ANATHEMA!

DAY 28

The clouds are particularly striking today. The sky is blue, the wind is gentle, the sea is calm, and I am sitting in the garden like Shakespeare's poor old Polonius, complacently imagining camels, elephants and such drifting through heaven above me. I was not always such a sucker for clouds, though. It is only lately that I have come to consider them vital components of the natural order – not just in a scientific or climatic sense, which they self-evidently are, but as immanent contributors to the idea of things.

The reason I used to dismiss them as mere grace notes, so to speak, was this: it was obvious to me that when they appeared in landscape paintings by even the greatest of artists, they were not as they really appeared. Obviously not, I thought. Long before your Constable or your Canaletto had completed his masterpiece, the clouds had moved on. They were, so to speak, phony accessories. This I easily confirmed because, as it happens, I have facsimile sketchbooks by both those masters, and by comparing preparatory sketches with completed works, I could confirm that the clouds in them were not, as it were, painted from the life.

But then, I thought, this was not the clouds' fault. Perhaps there was indeed a moment when they looked as dramatic as they did around Constable's Salisbury Cathedral, or really did hover so languidly above

Canaletto's Grand Canal. So then I recognized them not as shams, but as collaborators. As the personality of a great conductor contributes, centuries later, to the genius of a Beethoven, so those clouds, however arbitrarily they are appended to a landscape, add to nature's own grand work of art a grace note of human imagination.

DAY 29

There are many weaknesses, I admit, to the romantic temperament. On TV the other day an American woman was talking about America's gun laws, and she very nearly converted me to her point of view. She spoke of her people as being ready always to defend themselves against evil and stand up for their freedom and their way of life, the future of their children, their pride in their past, defending their heritage if necessary by force of arms, yessir. By golly, I admired her for it. It sounded fine to me.

She quoted, of course, the Second Amendment to the US Constitution, AD 1789, part of the Bill of Rights, so I looked it up in my copy of that document and found that it simply says this: 'A well regulated Militia, being necessary for the security of a free State, the right of the people to keep and bear Arms, shall not be infringed.' It seems to me that the purpose of this decree was the security of the infant State itself, without a standing army, and I am fairly sure that the Founding Fathers, three centuries ago, did not foresee a society with a revolver under every pillow, let alone an automatic rifle in the wardrobe or a pink gun for women. That lady's rhetoric fired me for a time, before I checked her references, and there's the weakness of the romantic temperament.

So often bad things have an alluring side to them, and it's the allure that first attracts people like me. War is vile,

49

but all too often I tend to concentrate upon its concomitants of courage, loyalty and sacrifice. I enjoy the swank and glory of the old British Empire, but I know very well that it was founded upon fundamental injustice. I am often entertained by the goings-on of petty criminals, and even find myself momentarily in sympathy with towering villains – wasn't there an undeniable splendour to those ghastly Nuremberg parades, or a sort of fascination to the creepy mass demonstrations of North Korea? I have even written a little book celebrating the Second World War Japanese battleship *Yamato*, although I know full well that the ship was the ultimate symbol of a crazed and often horribly cruel regime.

But there we are. The point of my *Yamato* book is the infinite irony of war, and the weakness of my temperament is a tendency to get priorities confused.

DAY 30

The sea! The sea! There is a place on the A497, not far from my house, where motorists coming from England can see at last, as they cross a gentle mound in the road, the waters of Cardigan Bay. If there are children in the car, as likely as not it is the very first time that they have set eyes on the sea, and I love to see them as they pass, jumping up and down with excitement and crying (I love to suppose), 'Thalassa! Thalassa!', as did Xenophon's Greeks when they reached the shore of their homeland at last.

I know just how they felt, both the Greeks and the children. I have lived almost all my life beside the sea. Most of the books I have written have been about sea cities – Venice, Manhattan, Sydney, Trieste – and I always felt, writing about dear old Oxford, that the one thing it lacked was a beach. The sea itself was a sort of homeland for me, and nowadays I can hardly imagine life far from a shoreline – life without an open border, without a horizon, as it were, without that sense of wider meanings that the ocean provides (for look at the globe and you will realize that all the seas are but one ocean, interconnected throughout, with the land mass only a vast archipelago within it).

To be honest, I have never read Xenophon, so it has ignorantly occurred to me to wonder, as I write this piece, which was the particular bit of sea that his Greeks reached that day two thousand years ago. I had always assumed

51

that it was the Aegean, or the Ionian, or some other part of the Mediterranean that was as home to them as the Irish Sea is to me. It was not. It was the Black Sea, a long way from Athens and hardly more than a great lake, like a bigger Caspian. For a moment, I thought perhaps I was wrong in my romantic interpretations of Thalassa.

But no, I should have known better. I looked again at my own globe, and of course there at the bottom of the Black Sea was the lesser Sea of Marmara, and at the bottom of that the fateful strait of the Dardanelles, which connected its waters, uninterrupted, not just with the Aegean or the Mediterranean, but with all the other seas everywhere on earth, even sending a drop or two, I like to suppose, together with a fraternal whisper of Xenophon, to the far waters of Cardigan Bay, which I can see from my window as I write.

DAY 31

Scenes of Family Life! These are a dozen events, major and minor, experienced or reported, that have just happened to us in our old age:

(1) A daughter complained, almost in tears, that the work on her house had been wretchedly half completed.

(2) A son reported, almost in despair, an unwelcome development in his marital affairs.

(3) A grandson said he would like to murder the man who invented homework.

(4) A son sent us a poster of his poetical and musical festival in the Alpujarra mountains.

(5) A son sent us a photograph of a horned owl in his garden in Alberta.

(6) A daughter sent us animal pictures she had taken in Kenya.

(7) A grandson sent us underwater photographs he took in Portsmouth harbour.

(8) A son left on the kitchen table a delicious risotto to heat up for our supper.

(9) A (very small) granddaughter knocked on the door with a peculiar cake she had made with her own hands.

(10) A (larger) granddaughter reported that her new school wasn't too bad after all.

(11) A ginger cat popped in from somewhere. Nothing to
do with us.
(12) A son popped in too, out of the dusk, just to see if we
were OK.

So it goes, the diurnal sequence, bad and good, happy
and unhappy, to outlast us in all our generations.

DAY 32

A Touching Poem for Monday Morning

In the north part of Wales there resided, we're told,
Two elderly persons who, as they grew old,
Being tough and strong-minded, resolute ladies,
Observing their path towards heaven or Hades,
Said they'd still stick together, whatever it meant,
Whatever bad fortune, or good fortune, sent.
They'd rely upon Love, which they happened to share,
Which went with them always, wherever they were.
And if it should happen that one kicked the bucket,
Why, the other would simply say 'Bother!'
(Not 'F--- it!' for both were too ladylike ever to
  swear . . .)

DAY 33

Years ago I happened to see across the street in an English country town an elderly widower I had known long before in Africa. He was carrying a shopping bag and was anxiously consulting what I took to be his shopping list, before stumbling shortsightedly into a nearby supermarket. I was greatly touched, because not so very long before I had known him in the strong prime of his manhood, the governor of an imperial province and master of a hundred thousand fates.

But it was not just that I saw in him an allegory of history, symbolizing the end of an ideology and the discrediting of a tremendous conviction. No, I realized there and then that I was foreseeing a tragedy that befalls millions of us, when we are obliged to realize, like Shakespeare's Othello, that our life's purpose is gone. Othello's purpose, of course, was the winning of battles, but for most of us it is nothing so finite, just the satisfaction of doing a job as well as we can do it. I once described the city of Trieste, a place I love, as having sadly lost its purpose, and a reader wrote to say that I had defined his own situation exactly, as a once busy man in retirement.

Do we not know them – the dedicated teachers without pupils, the builders without orders, the lawyer without a brief, the shopkeeper without a shop, the doctor without a patient? Of course, many of them enjoy worthwhile retirements, with family responsibilities or creative hobbies, but it seems to me that only one intangible, religious faith apart, can be relied upon to see us happily through our last years. It is Art, which is infinite in itself, which can be creative or comforting, active or passive, which comes from nowhere, which goes everywhere, which is omniscient, which is laughter and pity and puzzle and beauty, which is equally available to all of us, practitioners or recipients, and which can satisfy all our senses while the going is good.

I do hope the ex-imperialist I saw that day went home, his chores done and his purpose fulfilled, to write another chapter of his memoirs, or at least to hear some Mozart on his wind-up gramophone.

DAY 34

Here's a small device I employ for the entertainment of the nations – and myself. I am attracted by cars, and when I see an interesting one pull up beside me in a car park I jump out of my old Honda and prepare to accost the owner of the Jaguar or Aston Martin purring there beside me, or the sporty convertible still ticking over. Its owner, and even more noticeably his wife, view me with distaste as I approach them. They think I am going to remonstrate with them in some way, for selfish driving perhaps, or unauthorized parking, or show-off vulgarity, or any of a thousand possibilities of bureaucratic or politically correct interference. I can see them, as they half get out of their own car, preparing some perfectly justified retort of annoyance.

But no. What I say to them is simply this: 'I want your lovely car. I'll swap you mine for it.' You will hardly believe what happy responses this simple deceit affords – the relief of it, of course, but also the pride of ownership and the harmless and, indeed, affectionate effrontery. We part like old friends, laughing still, all of us, as my old Type R blunders its way out of the car park.

DAY 35

Surveys show that in Birmingham, England, 89 per cent of persons between the ages of fifty-eight and ninety suffer from ingrowing toenails.

Well, they don't actually, so far as I know, but you must admit that the statistic rings perfectly true, so accustomed have we become to such preposterous reports. Sometimes they are comical, sometimes they are tragic, sometimes they sound suspiciously like advertising and sometimes they are surely of political purpose. The awful thing is that however improbable they seem to be, they might be true. Eighty-nine per cent of those persons in Birmingham may well have toenail trouble, and you and I have absolutely no way of checking.

The things they tell us, corroborated, of course, by statistics! We are told which States, provinces, regions or age groups are happiest (in 1945, it is perhaps worth recalling, 90 per cent of New Yorkers considered themselves happy). We learn for certain which brand of toothpaste is preferred by dentists. An academic survey declares that Edward Heath was the fifth-worst British prime minister since the Second World War. What proportion of infants in Asia are likely to grow up with intestinal deficiencies? By what majority did the government retain office in the Salukistan general election? (99.5 per cent.) How long do female sand eels live, on average? (Twenty-eight years and three months.)

Actually, I am not absolutely sure about the last one – I may be thinking of camels – but you will know what I'm trying to say. In my opinion, statistical surveys are not just a bane of our lives, but downright manipulators. Take us or leave us, they tell us, but I think they are just one more symptom of a society, or a civilization, that is losing its sense of give and take.

Oh, the world is sometimes an old bore, I thought to myself as, mulling over these annoyances, I drove home this evening. But just then there reached me over the car radio a recording of Dianne Reeves singing, to the accompaniment of Romero Lubambo's guitar, the bittersweet song 'Darn That Dream'. Remember it? I loved hearing it again, was quite cheered up by it, and gave it 98.5 per cent in my inner statistics, but I dare say that if there were a poll about it in northern Nicaragua, approval would be unanimous.

Who are you to believe?

DAY 36

A visitor. An elderly, bearded, well-spoken stranger came to my door carrying a sheaf of papers. He said he wanted to read me a poem he had written, so I invited him in, and he read it to me. Well, he said, what did I think of it? I said I was really no judge of poetry and I could hardly take it in first time round, but it did seem to have a sense of power to it. So he gave me a copy of it, we talked for a quarter of an hour, and he went on his way.

This encounter has had a powerful effect on me, for he turned out to be no passing nut or charlatan, but a retired nuclear engineer who had worked in power stations for decades; and his poem, when I read it to myself, was indeed powerful, for it was a masked warning against the evils and dangers of everything nuclear. He was, it seemed, dedicating his retirement to waking the world to them, in poesy as in argument.

Cheerfully enough, but seriously, he worked upon me. He talked to me about nuclear leaks and earth contaminations, diseased animals, Hiroshima and Nagasaki, submarines, faulty power stations, wasted tidal power, disarmament and over-armament, the purposes of war and chances of peace . . .

And so on . . . I knew most of it already, but such was his earnest power, and so scholarly and kindly his manner, that when he went I was left in a kind of daze. I saw him

to the gate, and then I sat down, read his poem again and
wrote this piece.

DAY 37

O there's a lot to be said for Australia! I was not always loved there, because long years ago I expressed the opinion that Sydney was . . . But times have changed since then, and so have I, and in writing a more mature later book I discovered how much I was under the strange spell of the place.

In those days of my youth, Australia was essentially a distant, ex-British, provincial kind of country. Now it is among the prodigies. Its actors and writers are known the world over. Its sportsmen are brilliant. Its armed forces are universally respected. Its TV programmes are showing at this moment in households across the world. In modern times has any nation of only 21 million souls been quite so pre-eminent?

It is true that the Australian brush-turkey may still be encountered strolling in some provincial city streets, true too that there are blemishes to Australia's racial record – but then, which among all the nations has the right to call that particular kettle black? (Oops, watch it, political correctness . . .)

For metropolitan maturity, anyway, I draw your attention to two recent examples of official Australian *savoir faire*. In 2016, Australia Post, at last delivering a postcard that had been posted ten years before, politely apologized for any inconvenience caused by the delay, while a motion proposed in the distinguished upper house of the New South Wales parliament, also in 2016, described Donald Trump, at that moment the Republican candidate for the presidency of the United States, as a revolting slug.

The motion was carried unanimously.

DAY 38

I happened to remember this morning a crude and graphic acronym from my soldiering days: SNAFU, meaning Situation Normal: All Fucked Up. Just to confirm the contemporary truth of it, I have before me now one of the oldest and more temperate journals of the London press, and here are the news items I find spread across its domestic pages:

An eminent gent unjustly accused of child molestation says he is going to sue the police for false arrest. Thirteen years after the event, a sex gang rape victim (as the headline puts it) appears in court to see her eight molesters convicted. Scientists have taken tissues from the tail of a mouse, turned them into eggs, implanted them in another mouse and induced her to hatch eleven babies. A banker is caught laughing on TV as he 'pushes his face into a woman's breasts'. A man is arrested for alleged rape after a party inside the British Houses of Parliament. A multiple bigamist is found hanged after his third wife discovers he is courting a fourth. A con man relieves a seventy-eight-year-old pensioner of her £75,000 life savings by offering her 'a complete care package', treating her as his grandmother and promising her a cottage in Wales.

'O, the poor dear lady,' I can hear my own late mother murmuring from the afterlife. 'Whatever is the human race coming to?' But you haven't heard nothing yet, Mum.

Wait till you see the world news pages! And there, strewn across all of that stately broadsheet, is a single day's record of such depravity, misery, corruption, cruelty, greed and unkindness as would make Satan himself shudder. You might think the frightful tales of war and madness must be the worst part of it, but I myself am most sickened by the story of a captive chimpanzee, in a North Korean zoo, who has been trained to chain-smoke, gets through a pack a day, lights her own cigarettes and puffs away before enthusiastically laughing crowds of spectators.

'I give up at last,' my old mother would probably say (and just think, her only brother was killed and her husband horribly gassed in the First World War . . .).

DAY 39

It is only natural to complain of old age. I certainly do, and I grumble all too frequently about its miseries. However, senility can have advantages too. Do you remember that gifted English actor who, discovering that he was particularly adept at playing elderly parts, professed himself older than he really was – a deceit, revealed only at his death, that harmed nobody and amused all his admirers? Alas, my true age is all too obvious and known to all, but if I cannot exploit it for professional purposes, I find I am not above making personal use of it.

Dear me, when I think about it, how shameless I am! Graciously as any duchess do I accept the open door, the helping hand, the place in line, the kindly favour, the forgiveness of ineptitude. The thing is this: I am ninety-one years old, and that's past a Threshold. Ninety was a landmark, ninety-one the start of new privilege. Ninetys' Rights, that's my cause now, and this is a campaign song I've written for it:

> *Hail the old who all know best,*
> *The veterans who've passed the test,*
> *Pensioners of vast experience,*
> *Heroes beyond all interference!*
> *As moon must pale beside the sun,*
> *So it's the duty of every one*

To bow the knee or swiftly run,
To open the door or cock the gun
At the very presence of NINETY-ONE.
Ninety-One. Ninety-One. Open the door for
   Ninety-One!

(World rights: Senex and Sage, Llanystumdwy, Wales)

I like to think of myself as being beyond prejudice. I don't in the least mind people being white, black, yellow, brown – Christian, Buddhist, Muslim, atheist – posh, plebeian, boring, patronizing, impertinent – football fans, cricket bores, drug addicts, intrusive smokers, practical jokers, feminist extremists (within reason), male chauvinists (just) – thick as mutton, intolerably clever, humourless (at a pinch) or just indefinably unlikeable.

There are times, though, I am sorry to confess, when I find myself prejudiced against obesity, and I am genuinely ashamed of it. Obesity is caused by a variety of conditions, I well know – conditions psychological and physical, inherited and environmental – but I fear I generally attribute it, a priori, to plain overeating . . .

Of course, this is grossly unfair, and I suspect it sometimes goads the overweight themselves into an understandable suggestion of arrogance. They know what people like me are thinking, and I am truly sorry that we are. But there we are, my one and only Prejudice.

But here's a happy escape clause: the children of all the overweights I encounter seem to be, almost one and all, entirely delightful. Please, God, make the gross corpulence of our times be only a generational matter, and arrange in your mercy that all those reassuring children, when they grow up, are no more than plump, portly, broad in the beam and famously likeable.

DAY 41

Fact or fiction? As an old pro of the writing game, I don't recognize the distinction. The two kinds are irrevocably mingled in my own work, and to one degree or another, I suspect, in most other writers' work too. The thing is, truth is not absolute. It's all in the mind. For centuries it was absolutely true that the earth was flat, and only the other day I read as scientific fact that the universe was a hundred times bigger, or it may have been a thousand times bigger, than reference books had assured us for years. What's true to some people is untrue to others. What's true now may not be tomorrow, and vice versa. Just think, after all these centuries some people maintain that there is no such thing as God!

I do admit, though, that I have occasionally written things that are demonstrably, and permanently, untrue. Long ago I told a story about the great Sherpa climber Tenzing, and the pleasure he had from a very good claret at a State banquet I attended. This was absolutely untrue, as I discovered only recently, when I unearthed a menu of that very dinner and found that only burgundy had been served. Then again, I once reminisced romantically about an evening in Australia when the great wings of the Sydney Opera House (I wrote) soared like a benediction over our content. It did not soar over us at all, I later realized, because the Sydney Opera House hadn't been built yet.

But as for a subtler kind of truth, the inner kind that is seminal and personal to every one of us, I will defend to the death my right to exploit it. What I see in a picture, or a place, or a face, or even an event, is not necessarily what you see. It is my truth that I am recording. People sometimes complain to me about it. 'My memory of Oxford [or Trieste, or Rorke's Drift, or the Kentucky Derby],' they maddeningly say, 'is not in the least like the evocation of it in your book.' 'Well, of course it isn't,' I always feel like replying, 'you didn't write the book! My mind isn't your mind!'

But I never do. I know what they mean, the oafs.

DAY 42

I slept badly last night, having had trouble meeting the deadline for an essay I was writing, and so I fell into a sort of half-dream, a technique I have evolved for the purposes of recording these Thoughts.

I imagined myself seeing the earth as a whole, as astronauts do from space, and layer by layer, as I approached it, analysing its condition. First there was a universal stratum of decline – the general corruption of air and atmosphere, the filth of the seas, the vanishing wildlife and all that. Then, a layer down, I reached the frightful confusion of human enmities that seemed to be becoming permanent, with all its ancillaries of racism and spite, from refugee drownings to nuclear threats, starvation to cruelty to plain bigotry. Closer to home, what decency could I see down there? Only a welter of political and financial ambition, greed, moral degradation, a morass of uncertainty enveloping all the nations and fostering bitterness everywhere, in democracies as in despotisms.

And, finally, I reached my own sweet home, among my friends, in the country I loved. And I forgot about my unfinished essay then, turned over and went to sleep.

DAY 43

'Home, James, and don't spare the horses.' The phrase pursued me for years, in the days when I was still called James myself, and it made me wonder how many of the catchphrases of my time are still active, or even remembered. 'Home, James', I discovered, has got into the dictionaries, if only because legend attributes it to Queen Victoria, addressing a favoured coachman. But there must have been many more, especially in the adolescent years of radio and television, which entered the language from showbiz or America, and must surely have entered my own lingo. Are they still hanging around?

It is certainly true that if I say to my twelve-year-old granddaughter 'See you about, trout', she may well retort 'See you later, alligator', but I am fairly certain that if I said to somebody 'Cheerio', I would not get the retort 'Pip, pip', which was common enough in my youth. What about 'spot on', meaning 'exactly so', or 'step on it' or 'super', or 'wizard' as an exclamation of delight? Gone, all gone, I suspect – or did suspect until a moment ago, when the *Oxford Dictionary* assured me that 'wizard', though dated, could still just mean 'wonderful'. (It recognizes 'lingo' too . . .)

But anyway, if phrases fade, so does the excitement of new things and new ideas. Where, for example, are the pressure cookers of yesterday's kitchens? What happened to the hovercraft, that marvel of engineering, so magnificently splashing its way from Dover to Calais? Your old snaps from the Polaroid, not so long ago a miracle of modernity, are browning now in forgotten drawers, and so are the elegant playing cards and stationery items that they used to dish out on that lost Monarch of the Skies, the Concorde. Gone, all gone, such ikons of yesteryear, and it won't be long, I fear, before we say farewell to that virtuoso performer of punctuation, that champion of the Individualist Style, the Exclamation Mark.

RIP to all of them, every one!!!!

DAY 44

There is much to be said for nostalgia. It can be debilitating, I know, but it can be agreeable too, especially when one reaches the years of discretion, and I spend much of my time wallowing in it.

In misty panorama the years and the places pass through my inner vision, and I remember events I have completely forgotten, see cities I can no longer identify, and even sense lost fragrances and seminal emotions. One of the pleasures of nostalgia, indeed, is the pleasure of chasing one's memories. Memories, memories! They may be blurred, but they can be vivid too, and they can trigger long-lost associations. Only today there suddenly came into my mind a forgotten name – just a name. I can hardly spell it, let alone pronounce it properly, but it instantly summoned into my nostalgia a barrack room of some sort in Egypt long ago. I was among a group of foreign correspondents, from all over the world, covering some Middle Eastern crisis or other, and with that misty name some music came to me too. It was a popular song of the time, 'Just One of Those Things', and it was jauntily sung with a fairly mangled lyric by – by – by – who was it, who was it? Yes, got it, I remember. It was Nate Poliwetzky, if that's how he spelt the name. Nate Poliwetzky, or perhaps Poliwesjzi, of AP, or UP, or AFP, or one of the other news agencies, and I can see him now in full performance, far away in time and place, half a lifetime ago. How we laughed! How we sang!

That's what nostalgia can do. If you're still around, Nate Poliwetzky, sing that song again for me, will you?

DAY 45

What is it with the birds? What are they on about? How do they steer? What are they up to? Who runs them? I can't make them out at all.

This morning, I walked along the edge of a tidal meadow near our place, half grassland, half saltwater pools, and there I came across a multitude of Canada geese, plus a few whooper swans, all nibbling away at the grass in frenzied unison, as it were. After lunch, I went back to take another look at them, and lo! – every single one of those creatures, every one of those twitching, nibbling bundles of bird had vanished.

Where had they gone? Who ordered them to go? Where had they come from? Why did they come here? Who marshalled them? Why?

I don't really want to know. I'm very pleased that they did come, and flattered that they should have flown, in their elegant V-formation, I assume, halfway across the world to our particular corner of another continent. I am glad that, so far as I know, years of scientific research, by generations of specialists, have not revealed to us (or to me, anyway) how birds work, how they remember those immense migratory journeys, how they know when to change course, or even how the half-dozen crows on the telegraph wire outside our house suddenly and unanimously decide, one and all, to take off and go home.

I spent an evening once at a shearwater colony in Australia, watching the little birds, as night fell, unerringly flying back to their own particular burrow in the dusk. Not a flicker of hesitation, not a single second thought, only swift, sudden swoops out of the sky on to the sand and into the underground. And I was proud to think that perhaps the most famous of all shearwaters should have been at least part-time Welsh. The small island of Ynys Enlli, Bardsey to the English, is almost within sight of my home, and it was the destination of the longest avian flight itinerary ever recorded – the half-century career of a Manx shearwater which, in its annual migrations between Cardigan Bay and the coast of South America, flew a million miles, or ten times to the moon and back.

What an impertinence, to ask it how it was done! No, let all the birds, big and small, friendly or aloof, keep their grand mysteries to themselves and leave us simple humans marvelling.

DAY 46

I am happily susceptible to the abstraction the Welsh call *hiraeth*. Dictionaries define it simply as longing, but to Welsh poets down the generations it has meant far, far more. The fourteenth-century master Dafydd ap Gwilym, for instance, declared it variously the Son of Memory, the Son of Intention, the Son of Grief and the Son of Enchantment. Fortunately, the conception has always treated me kindly, and twice, in the course of my daily exercise, it has given me a moment of epiphany – a brief lovely conviction that all would eventually be well, for me and for all others, as the old world turned again.

And lo, it happened to me once more today as I walked up our lane. I paused for a moment to take in the beauty of the morning – blue, blue sky with soft and genial clouds, two high trails of aircraft hastening romantically to the west, a dusting of snow on the mountains, a squawking of rooks somewhere and fifty-nine sheep (I counted them) speckling the Parrys' fields all around. Eureka!

Hiraeth!

When I got home, I found an e-mail from America, almost despairing at the miseries of everything – terminal depression, my friend thought, in a devastated country 'spinning downward'. I replied at once, with a loving message that all shall be well, all shall be very well, straight from the Son of Enchantment.

DAY 47

Last night, at the house Trefan Morys in Wales, we saw the Burning of the Books.

Doesn't the very phrase strike a chill down the spine and raise hideous images in the mind? Those dim burly figures prancing in the firelight? Those ghastly connotations of bullies, bigots and evil ideologies? Surely the burning of books anywhere, the symbolic shredding of the human mind's own sacred liberties, is as unforgivable at Trefan Morys as it was in Berlin long ago?

But hang about. I have better excuses than the Nazis did. It was very cold at Trefan Morys last night, and I was disconcerted to discover, as darkness fell, that we were entirely out of logs for our wood-burning Norwegian stove. What to do, when we all began to shiver and even the stove itself seemed to be looking back at me sadly?

I am not one of those enviable colleagues whose books, their publicity people tell us, have been translated into fifty or sixty foreign languages. No such luck. However, I have been printed in a few, and when this happens their obliging publishers always send me four or five copies for my own gratification. I add one at once to the row of my Collected Works, where everyone can see it and I can gloat over it in private. Other copies I give to the French, Italian, German or Spanish people who happen to turn up here in remotest Wales and might like a souvenir of their experience in their own tongue.

But I am left with translations into scripts that are as meaningless to me as they would be to my friends, neighbours and casual visitors – unwanted even by any second-hand booksellers or charity shops or indigent public libraries within a hundred miles of Llanystumdwy. So these unhappy volumes, often very handsome but with scripts back to front, or from top to bottom, or apparently upside down, in unrecognizable letterings and languages, and only a grinning photograph of yours truly on the back cover to identify them even to me – these poor victims of ethnicity end up in a black plastic container called the Disposal Box.

And from there last night, while the Welsh wind blew and the owls hooted, they suffered the Burning of the Books. I mourned for them as they flickered and blazed there, disintegrating before my eyes, and this morning the grey pile of their ashes, already cold in the grate, reproaches me in unknown tongues.

DAY 48

In all the anthologies of verse that I have in my library, few lines have more persistently pleased me than a little lyric written by Dorothy Fields in 1928, supposedly after overhearing a young New Yorker saying to his girl, as they looked longingly into Tiffany's jewellery window on Fifth Avenue, 'Gee, honey, I'd like to get you a sparkler like that, but right now I can't give you nothin' but love.'

Everything about this little anecdote seems to me just perfect (especially when it's linked to the catchy tune that Jimmy McHugh wrote for it back then, and which I can still whistle for you, if you like). It is so absolutely of its period, from the argot of the young man ('Gee, honey', 'sparkler', 'right now') to the social implications (the Great Depression of the 1920s) and the underlying All-Americanness of it (in a 1931 movie the song was sung as a duet by Mickey and Minnie Mouse).

For of course those lines could only come from America, and from an America of a particular period, before true greatness set in, and disillusionment. As it happens, I met Dorothy Fields before she died in 1974, and I have always been sorry that she does not figure in the *Oxford Book of American Light Verse*. Never mind, in 2009 the 44th President of the United States, in his inaugural speech, quoted some more immortal lines of hers – not the ones

about nothing but love, but the ones about picking ourselves up and dusting ourselves down . . .

DAY 49

Spur of the Moment

This morning, as I began my breakfast, a kind e-mail reached me from foreign parts. A few moments before, I suppose, an old friend had read something of mine in a newspaper. He told me that he was sitting in a transit lounge at Changi airport in Singapore, just in from Yangon (where's that?) and waiting for a flight to London, and he was surrounded by whimpering children and their doubtless exhausted mums. I know the scene too well! But at once, there and then, having read those unimportant paragraphs in the paper, he had sent me an appreciative message on his iPad.

Isn't spontaneity wonderful? That touching little communication meant far more to me because he had written it there and then, impulsively, on the spur of the moment. Nothing is less convincing, in my view, than the previously prepared compliment, unless it is the odiously practised witticisms of politicians or, dear me, the traditional funny bits in the best man's encomium. Even many professional comedians, the ones that obviously have joke books or assistants, sound to me all too rehearsed; only the true masters, seldom your standard TV clowns, display the true genius of quip and repartee.

Anyway, when I got that delightful message over my

cornflakes this morning I spent half an hour fashioning a suitable response, but decided in the end upon 'Thanks a lot. Love Jan.'

DAY 50

'Let us now praise Famous Men.' Who wrote that, and why? It seems to me that all too many famous men are soon forgotten, and often deserve to be . . .

Sixty or seventy years ago, when I was a young and footloose journalist, I stuck in a scrapbook page pictures of Famous people I had met in the short course of my career, and now here the page is before me. Fifty people (only one a woman!) are immortalized there in fading photographs or cartoons – statesmen, rulers, politicians and miscellaneous magnates, with a few artists and sportsmen. I wonder how many are Famous still, or will be much longer?

The Queen of England, of course, is Famous *ex officio* – Elizabeth II until the end of history. So are one or two of the American presidents. T. S. Eliot is certainly not forgotten, and nor is Walt Disney, but what about those transient swells and potentates, those Luces and Onassises, Dr Moussadeks, Crown Prince Abdullah, Shepilov?

Shepilov? Who was Shepilov? Famous in his time, evidently, or he wouldn't be in my scrapbook, but like many another, his light must have flickered and faded even before the old reaper came round.

PS By the way, the man who told us to praise Famous Men was the anonymous biblical author of the Book of Ecclesiasticus (as against the Book of Ecclesiastes), who included, incidentally, among the exemplary champions of his Chapter 44 people who 'find out musical tunes, and recite verses in writing'.

PPS I never met President Kennedy, but I attended one of his political rallies, and reported to the *Guardian* my prescient instinct that he would never grow old. Alas, I never met Leonard Cohen either, but I did once meet his mother.

PPPS You think I'm rambling rather? So?

DAY 51

Half a century in cricketing terms, nearly seven weeks of my Thoughts! And today I wish to pay a tribute to Progress. The world is too much with us, God knows, but there is one implement of the new age that seems to me a blessing: the electronic tablet, which has become not just a useful tool to me, but a true benediction, and should in my opinion be made available, by government decree, to every citizen from birth to death, especially to inmates of HM prisons and the terminally lonely.

Just think! Only yesterday I wanted to confirm the origin of a particularly obscure biblical phrase, not included in my Oxford reference books. Not only was it there on my iPad, large as life, with sundry side references too, but before I returned to my desk I was able, almost without trying, to see and hear Daniel Barenboim playing a Beethoven sonata in a palace somewhere in the 1950s. I could just as easily have switched for a laugh with the late Tommy Cooper, or played a game of solitaire, or found a recipe for a goat-cheese quiche, or consulted the opinions of the world's best doctors about excessive urination, or, for that matter, sent a small contribution to the lifeboats.

The world was certainly with me, but not in Wordsworth's dire sense. On the contrary, such worldly blessings were available to me, thanks to a later technical revolution than his, as would have made his heart sing! Just think

89

what happiness a tablet must offer to bed-ridden people, or the lonely, or the imprisoned, or even simply the bored stiff. It is, in my view, one of the truly welcome instruments of Progress – even of Happiness, even of Kindness itself, that ultimate abstraction!

A Morning Limerick

Not feeling terribly bright,
I lost all compunction to write.
Without more inquiry
I shut up my diary
And read P. G. Wodehouse all night.

DAY 52

A greetings card arrived the other day picturing five cats all in a row, two black-and-white, three tabbies. They stare back at me now, and honorary cat that I like to think myself, I am fascinated by the different expressions in their eyes. The black-and-white ones, which seem to be animals of the fluffy, bedroom-slipper kind, appear properly conformist and look back at me without much interest, satisfied, kindly enough – not unlike, in fact, the artificial cats' eyes that line our country streets as safety devices. In the eyes of the three tabbies, though, there is an expression at once melancholy and eager, with a touch of the wild perhaps.

My family and I have lived with generations of cats, from reckless Siamese on our houseboat on the Nile to sturdy extra-toed characters (like Ernest Hemingway's in Key West). One among them all has looked back at me with an expression altogether different, the look of an equal. He was a Norwegian Forest cat, of a breed until recently unrecognized as a pedigree – no more than working farm cats. I named him Ibsen for his national origins, and went to Norway once especially to see his kind on the job. He was big and handsome and thoroughly decent, and until the day he died I considered him a friend and a colleague.

He was the last of our cats. We shall never have another, but I often think of him, and share a chuckle, when I pass a road sign, half hidden by foliage, which has for months ineffectually tried to warn us of a missing traffic aid ahead.

'WARNING!' it appears to proclaim. 'NO CATS'.

DAY 53

'I'll Have a Damned Good Try'

It seems to me that catchphrases or odd quotations catch the essential character of a people better than national anthems. Just the single line 'sea to shining sea' perfectly articulates the native American sense of greatness, just as '(I'm a) Yankee Doodle Dandy' is just right for its cockiness. Two words – *Marchons! Marchons!* – are all we really need of the 'Marseillaise', and who's going to thrill to 'Australia the beautiful' when Matilda waltzes merrily by? 'Danny Boy' is Ireland, for me anyway, a snatch of 'Lily Marlene' is enough to transport me sentimentally to Berlin, and I know people who think the voice of a gondolier singing 'O sole mio' is the true voice of Italy herself.

As for England, two lines in particular seem to me truer to the nation than 'God Save the Queen'. One is 'It's being so cheerful as keeps us going,' a governing catchphrase of the Second World War. The other comes from 1916, when during the calamitous landings at Gallipoli Brigadier General Henry Napier approached in his boat the ghastly beach of Sedd el Bahr, already littered with the dead and wounded, and raked by Turkish machine guns.

'Go back, sir,' his soldiers shouted, 'go back, you can't land!'

94

'I'll have a damned good try!' the general said, and perhaps that's not bad for a national text. He was killed before he got ashore.

DAY 54

From the Innocent Long Ago

I pick up a newspaper, and tell myself yet again that Thomas Rowlandson has a lot to answer for. Yes, I know he died in 1827 (I've just looked it up) and that he was a considerable illustrator and portraitist in his day, besides being a great caricaturist. To my mind, though, he is responsible for the degradation of British political cartoons today. Not long ago they were often caustic, witty, beautifully drawn, instantly understandable and relevantly funny.

Today, it seems to me, the Rowlandson legacy has been tiresomely degraded. His technique combined meticulous draughtsmanship and design with what was then, I imagine, a marvellously shocking degree of coarseness. The balance was more satire than farce, but only just.

Alas, his disciples two centuries later are all too wedded to the cruder aspects of his genius, and today's English political cartoons, even those commenting upon grand or terrible events of contemporary history, are all too likely to be ornamented with the grotesqueries, farts and bare bums that doubtless meant more in the innocent long ago.

That's all. I can always throw it away, can't I?

DAY 55

It's cheating I know, but I can't resist rescuing from oblivion, for no particular reason, a ditty I wrote years ago that still amuses me. It is called 'Pig Rhyme', and this is how it goes:

A mother pig crooned to her sweet little piglets three:
Come, wipe all the mud from your trotters,
and if you are good, we'll see!
There may be a bucket of acorn swill for your tea!
Swill, said the piglets, acorn swill, oh wow!
Is that all you've got, you silly old sow?
The mother pig cried: But when I was wee
A bucket of swill was oh, such a treat for me!
On birthdays I had it, and when I was good as could
  be!
Big deal, said the piglets three.

DAY 56

It is wonderful, isn't it, how insistently the experience of The First Time loiters in the memory! I don't mean the grand initiations, of Love or Death or Revelation, but the mundane events of life that have never happened to you before. Some of these you may have forgotten entirely, but many more are there somewhere in your subconscious, slightly fictionalized down the years, perhaps. And here is an example of my own, plucked at last into a nonagenarian limelight!

When I was young, brash and short of cash I mocked the pretensions of haute cuisine and all that, and when my love and I went for a holiday in France we spent a week at a very modest *pension* in the hills of Haute-Savoie. The food was healthy, the wine was cheap, the ambience was very pleasant, the people were charming, and it cost us practically nothing. 'You see?' we said to each other. 'Who needs more?'

On the way out of the mountains, though, at the end of our stay, I happened to notice a sign announcing the presence of a celebrated lakeside restaurant which food snobs had bragged to me about. We had to admit it looked inviting. 'Oh well, hell,' we said to ourselves, 'just this once,' and in we went.

We ate a single dish of little fish fresh out of the lake, with a bottle of Sancerre, crispy rolls and coffee to conclude. It cost us more than the entire bill for our week's stay at the *pension*, food, beds and all.

It was my very first experience of a truly great French restaurant, and *mon dieu*, I have never looked back.

DAY 57

Most of us, I suppose, in these days of almost universal misery, must occasionally wonder what God is about – even agnostics like me who are not at all sure that there is a God. One Sunday, I heard on the radio an ingenious Christian apologist explain why his God of peace seems to be failing us abysmally.

It was like this, he said. The peace we prayed for was the wrong peace. When Jesus spoke of peace, he meant God's peace, not ours – a different class of aspiration, it seems, apparently beyond human definition or understanding, but all embracing.

Well, thought I to my sceptical self, that sounds to me very like my own conception of the ideal. Utter, absolute absolution! Why bother with a God who apparently needs definition, demands repentance and expects worship – worship! – and capital letters to His Name? Even expects wars on his behalf?

Many decent Christians, indeed, do go into battle, if only figuratively, in one of their grand old hymns – 'Onward, Christian Soldiers', for example, 'marching as to war', sung to a stirring rhythm at sacred gatherings with the very best of intentions . . .

Here is my own adaptation of it:

Onward, friends and neighbours, into the kindly sun,
Where we are paid-up members, each and every one.
We need no theologians, no doctrinal guff,
No military idioms, no sham repentance stuff –
We take the worthy with the nasty, the gentle with the
   rough.
The Absolute of Absolutes, Kindness is enough!

DAY 58

Don't you find that some memories stay in the mind far
more clearly than others – more meaningfully, more alle-
gorically perhaps? One such memory for me concerns
my very first flight in an aeroplane, which happened just
about seventy years ago. Imagine!

It was an ancient de Havilland Dragon Rapide biplane,
born in the 1930s, and I had hitched a ride in it from
Cairo to Alexandria on a brilliant Egyptian summer's
day. I remember the celestial space of it all up there,
experienced for the very first time. All was blue and white
around me! I remember the desert sand meeting the azure
Mediterranean far, far below, but what I remember most
clearly of all was the moment when, high above the delta,
suddenly both the engines cut out. All was silence, but
for creaking and the swoosh of the wind, and it did occur
to me that I might be about to die, dropping silently and
ominously into Egypt out of that splendid lucidity!

But after a few minutes, the pilot turned around to me.
'Just saving a bit of fuel,' he shouted over his shoulder,
before starting the engines again, and that moment has
never left me. The irony of it, the shame (for I really was
frightened), the touch of comedy and the beauty – a brief
instant, that was all, set against so glorious and fateful
a landscape in so absolute a silence. When I recall the
moment, even now, I still feel some transcendental tremor,

as if that pilot had himself been obeying the edict of some more senior captain, assessing me. I failed the test, I fear, because of that moment of cowardice, but perhaps I have made up for it by remembering the moment to this very day with such a rich mixture of emotions!

DAY 59

Some thoughts today about sentimentality. Yesterday evening, I went to my copy of Dr Johnson's dictionary, fifth edition, 1788, bound in red leather, near mint condition, and as always when I pulled out Volume 2 I noticed once again the scuffed damage on its spine where, fifty years ago, my darling daughter, from her pram parked beside the bookcase, had picked away at its leather, throwing the bits on the floor and seriously reducing the value of the book (which had been given to me by my brother Gareth to celebrate the first ascent of Mount Everest).

Mingled reactions, then. I was wryly amused by the cost of that incident, elated as always by my love for Suki (who has long since had expensive babies of her own), proud and grateful for the memory of Gareth (died 2007), and warmed as always when I was reminded of Ed Hillary, Tenzing, the Western Cwm and all that . . . Add all those emotions up, though, examine them coolly, and I have to admit that I was being sentimental.

'Well, why not?' I hear you ask, and I agree with you. Not everyone will. Being sentimental, to many people nowadays, means being slushy or maudlin, and of course I see their point and know what they mean. My trouble is, though, that what they see as maudlin or slushy, I very often see simply as – well, full of sentiment. I admit that my experience with the dictionary extracted from me a slushy tear, and I am susceptible to melodies of facile emotion, like national anthems, love lyrics or novellas that sterner critics would despise. I would argue, though, that sentimentalism as such can only be good. Nobody calls you sentimental if you enjoy horror movies, however skilful they are, but they do if you admire Rupert Brooke; to shed a tear over a weepie movie is sentimental, to applaud a savage uppercut in a heavyweight contest certainly isn't.

In short, to my mind sentimentalism is properly only an excess of feeling, and there is certainly nothing wrong with that; it is false sentimentalism, pretending to have feelings that you don't really have, exaggerated emotions and trumped-up tears that should really be exorcised. As sense is to sensibility, so sentiment is to sentimentalism. Sterne meant what he said when he called his book *A Sentimental Journey*. So did Sinatra (by proxy, anyway) when he told us he was gonna make one. And so did I, when a tear came into my eye last night beside the bookcase downstairs.

By the way, I was consulting Dr Johnson's volume M–Z to find his definition of the word 'sentimentalism', but he doesn't even recognize it.

DAY 60

I am pleased to see on the Web that there are three sheep in Wales for every one human – not quite such a happy condition as New Zealand's, where the ratio is apparently four to one, but still comforting in a way. I am not a great admirer of sheepness, or sheepity, but I like to think that throughout our green and pleasant land, paradise to industrial valleys, for every one of us scheming, selfish and conceited humans there are three creatures genuinely, as the hymnists say, meek and mild.

But then again, while lambs are perfectly lovely in their playfulness, prettiness and innocence, they grow up to be less than enchanting. Are any of God's creatures more boring than your average adult sheep, permanently chewing the grass or the cud, apparently without a spark of ambition, night and day, night and day, for ever and ever feeding themselves and relieving themselves towards the end of life? Meek and mild, yes – once their parenting days are over they are apparently without responsibilities or ambitions, and there they are now outside my window, three of them to one of me, doing nothing at all but eat.

Still, they are much less harmful than we are, and when they were lambs they were perfect. We all were, humans and animals every one – even baby crocodiles are rather sweet. So I was comforted, just for once, by a statistic on the morning news – three of them to one of us.

Why should innocence be so transient? Heaven only knows.

DAY 61

Contemplating the melancholy truth that all living creatures look more attractive when they are young, it nevertheless strikes me as odd that human beings down the centuries have tried to look less old than they really are. Animals of many species, I know, disguise their true appearances, for safety's sake or hunting advantage, but so far as I know they do not try to hide their ages (although absolutely anything is possible, I know, in the crazy domain of nature, where most creatures spend their entire lives simply not dying).

But humans, especially in recent times female humans, have expended time, ingenuity and creative gifts in trying to make themselves appear younger than they are – in short, generally speaking, more sexually attractive than they probably are. Look at all the ancient portrait figures – even mummies! – that have been prettied up with paintwork. Did it work? Was the ageing Cleopatra lovelier for her cosmetics? For that matter, are the sexual celebrities of our own time enhanced by their vastly expensive make-up?

I seriously doubt it, and I prophesy that before too long the chemical beauty enhancers of today, plastered on faces young (because they think it looks sexy) and old (because they think it makes them look young), will seem ridiculously dated. Already, it seems to me, many of the most truly beautiful women of our time wear little make-up, and the most gaudily touched-up young celebrities are beginning to seem not simply tasteless, but actually anachronistic.

So here's a proposal for the powers that be: slap an enormous Vulgarity Tax on all cosmetics, while the going is good. The profits will be enormous, and can be devoted to good works, the promotion of comic art and compensation for the dispossessed owners of zoos, when they are finally, thank the Lord, made illegal.

A Rhyme for Christmas

I said to the Spirit of Christmas,
Christmas is not for me.
I've had too much of the pudding,
I'm tired of the Christmas tree.
I've noticed all that, he answered. I've watched you,
*   and what do I see?*
A soured old grouch with a soured old look,
Perpetually reading some gloomy old book.
Take a grip on yourself – look at me!
I'm laughing and joking and dancing all day,
Cheerful whatever may come my way!
Never complaining, never a tear,
And especially today, this Great Day of the year!
Said I, if that's an alternative course,
I'd rather keep grousing, peevish and cross,
And if things get still worse I can always, perforce,
Share a pint and good grumble with old Santa Claus.

DAY 63

If you are of a certain age, the most potently emotive volumes in your library are likely to be its old address books. All my life, not going in for anything as grandiose as bookplates, I have made a point of writing in my books when and where I bought each one, and these few thousand modest inscriptions (for example, in tiny fountain-pen ink, 'Oxford, 1936', or, in bolder felt-tip, 'Jerusalem, 1947') stir my feelings to some degree. They are impotent, though, beside the entries in my successive discarded address books.

Faded, scribbled all over, sometimes in pencil, sometimes in blotched ink, with crossings-out and amendments everywhere, outdated telephone numbers and half-legible street names and code addresses and postal codes and outdated married names and crossed-out references and incomprehensible foreign reminders, sideways, upside down, sometimes in black ink, sometimes in green pencil – and peering everywhere through the chaos are the names of my acquaintances down the years. I imagine them nervously awaiting their rediscovery, or re-enactment, and they seem to me like so many neglected invalids, or even tattered ghosts.

Ghosts, of course, half of them are. But consider the faces that peer back at me now. What became of W, when last we parted? How went his life? X, of course, we all know about him, and love him still, despite his problems. Oh, how touching, to see the repeated changes and corrections in one old friend's address, but how reassuring to find that another, confidently recorded half a lifetime ago, hasn't shifted one iota since!

So it goes, sometimes making me laugh, sometimes making me cry, and sometimes driving me to the telephone to test if a number is still extant. It is a healthy corrective to my emotions to realize that across the world there may be people idly looking through their own discarded telephone books to see what became of me.

DAY 64

Here's a dual confession. Yesterday we met for lunch a group of eight delightful young visiting relatives. They had suggested eating at the one expensive seafront restaurant that we have in these parts, so I telephoned the management beforehand to make sure that after the meal the bill would be presented to me, and not to them. God knows I am not rich, but they were young working people and children, and I was sure that if I let them, they would do the paying. This made me feel deplorably self-righteous.

Well, all went well. The meal was excellent (especially the local mussels), the conversation was fun (the one small boy who was a bit bored sensibly went off to play solitary football outside), and over the coffee I surreptitiously slipped outside to pay the bill with my credit card. It was a lot of money, of course, but smug as I was, I did not for a moment resent it, and I asked the cashier to add a generous gratuity to say thank you for the service.

'We don't accept tips on credit cards,' she coldly said. 'Cash only.'

Something cracked inside me then. 'Too bad,' I lied to her, 'I don't have any cash,' and I stalked off disgruntled. For this ugly denouement to a happy event I blame partly the damned bureaucracy of it, if that's what it was, but chiefly myself, and today I am doubly self-chastened.

PS My grandson Sam, who once worked in a restaurant, tipped our kind waitress with cash when I had gone.

The merry actress Debbie Reynolds has died, but with her name one of my happier memories lives on. She became a star in 1952 by playing opposite Gene Kelly in the smash musical *Singin' in the Rain*, a film that's still delightful even now, and down the years she became for me a sort of spirit of Hollywood.

I never met her, but the star and studio system that had made her famous was in its prime when I first went to Hollywood. It was 1954, and I was buoyant myself with the international kudos of the successful Everest expedition the year before, which I had reported for the London *Times* in a much publicized scoop. Because of Everest I had introductions to many film people, and although I never met Reynolds herself, I see now that in a sense it was her Hollywood that I encountered.

Success was in the very air of the place! Hardly had I landed there than I took tea with a sort of earlier incarnation of Debbie Reynolds. The grand dame of Hollywood in those days was Mary Pickford, who lived in immense grandeur, guarded by snooty aides, but who turned out to be, over tea and cakes in her garden, a most kindly old-school hostess happily basking in her own legend. Almost as celestial was Walt Disney, of *Snow White* and *Bambi* and *Pinocchio*, who was just about to launch his world-changing Disneyland, and he went to great trouble explaining to me how his cartoon chipmunks conversed (in English, played extremely fast backwards). I met the Oscar-winning art director of *Gone with the Wind*, then the most profitable movie ever made, and he and his wife took me to a local bingo club, where he won a prize of one dollar. I remember to this day the modest diffidence with which he accepted it when it was presented to him in the bottom of a goldfish bowl, and how genuinely pleased he was! These Hollywood eminences were good people, I swear, and so were the Hollywood technicians I met, the cameramen and the floor managers and the audio men and the electricians, ladies and gentlemen one and all, and true craftspeople.

All in all, then, I took to Hollywood 1954 – the Holly-wood of Debbie Reynolds and *Singin' in the Rain* and *Gone with the Wind* and the chattering chipmunks – as I took to the America they represented. Now that Debbie has left us, and her America too, I remember them one and all with fondness, gratitude and sad admiration.

DAY 66

Yesterday I realized that I lived in the best place on earth.

It was a glorious evening of early winter, a time of wondrous colouring – golds and greys and vermilions and deepest blues, interspersed and overlaid by towering structures of white clouds – a majestic kind of evening, across which evening seabirds elegantly flew.

Against this background you must imagine our landscape, as I experienced it breathless last night. To our south we see the Irish Sea in the evening tide, languidly rolling with its gentle line of spray, and beside it the long grey-blue line of the hills, speckled with farms and seashore houses, away down towards Carmarthen and Pembrokeshire beyond, and dimly guarded – can you see it? Just beyond the point there? – by the proud silhouette of Harlech Castle, where Glyndŵr of Wales fought the thievish English (and both sides still sing about it).

Turn around now, look to the north. Higher by far, and statelier, are the mountains of Snowdonia, striding down to the bay across the water meadows of Glaslyn. A more sombre green and brown those highlands are, with patches of slate, and in my heightened condition they seem to me to be playing solemn music up there, melodies drifting distantly around Snowdon itself, the home of the gods. Ah, and to complete the scene, do you see, through the gap beside the Moelwyns there, beyond the patch of forest, the first white gleam of the Welsh winter?

You think I am exaggerating the beauty of it all, and perhaps I am, but the true epiphany of that realization last night was not a physical vision at all. It was not an artistic experience, but rather the burst of conviction, as I stood above the bay there, that all around me that evening, away to the last twinkle of the remotest farmhouse light, there lived a community of generally decent people. There were rogues down there, of course there were, and fools, and no doubt whole-hog villains too; but I have lived a lifetime in this place, among these people of north-west Wales, contemplating such prospects in varying conditions of despair or exaltation, and I don't believe there is anywhere on earth better endowed with what I believe to be the ultimate beauty: the instinct of kindness.

Good morning!

DAY 67

I overheard a conversation in a café yesterday which pulled me up short. 'Do you like shortbread?' said one young man to another, and it was the reply that gave me a shock: 'Rather!' With its emphasis on the 'er' and its half-mouthful enthusiasm, it sounded to me like a retort from another age, from a P. G. Wodehouse dialogue perhaps. I hadn't heard it said for ages. And more disconcerting still, I realized it was the sort of thing I might well have said myself, fifty years ago!

How quickly a language changes, and with it the mores of a people, their tone of voice and their attitudes. In England, it seems to me, what they used to call Standard English does not greatly change, and that's what I speak myself. It's certainly not, though, what the Queen of England spoke sixty years ago. In her early broadcasts she sounded ineffably affected, and if her accent has changed over time, perhaps mine has too – we were born in the same year. Did I once talk a little like that? Did I employ usages like 'wait a mo', 'half a tick', 'you can say that again', 'top hole!' or even 'hot diggety dog'? Did I really say 'O rather!'?

My dear son Twm says nobody says that now, not even me, and he claims that I imagined hearing what that young man said in the shop. 'O shut your trap,' I tell him. 'Come off it.'

DAY 68

Here's a laugh! I used to love the dear old London *Times*, when I worked for it in the late years of its prime, and I still sometimes send things for publication in its letters page, as a useful medium of debate. They hardly ever get published, but the unused ones are still extant in my computer, and here are a few of them:

Sir: If schools are really to introduce the study of Atheism into their curricula, may I suggest a short course concerning Agnosticism? Lesson one, on Theological Theory: 'We don't know.' Lesson Two, on Universal Moral Application: 'Be Kind'.

Sir: Hooray! At last! Not a single picture of animals in captivity among today's illustrations!

Sir: Having lately been bemused by surveys concerning the relative likeableness of cities around the world, I resolved to keep my own register during a recent visit to London. During my two days here I conversed with 28 strangers – hotel workers, waiters, shop assistants, taxi-drivers and a couple of varied officials. Ten were European foreigners, four were Asians and one was a New Zealander. The only one who did not seem likeable, I am sorry to report, was a very English cab-driver, a class of Londoner I generally find delightful: but I was homesick by then and I expect he thought me nasty, too.

Sir: I am convinced my potted shrimps contain elements of sea-horse.

Sir: Is this not a moment for rational discussion about the future of the monarchy? We must all agree that we have been blessed by an admirable figurehead in Elizabeth 2, and most of us enjoy the pageantry, tradition and symbolism that attends the throne. However the idea of inherited power and privilege – pot-luck authority – has surely had its day. May I suggest, then, that instead of an all too human man or woman as the allegorical symbol of the State, the kingdom adopt the Crown itself? It can be surrounded by just the same aura of myth and majesty, conveyed in processions in golden coaches, attended by clip-clopping cavalry, blessed by archbishops, marvellous in its ancient meaning, but stripped of sycophancy and burdened by no rash assumptions of virtue or ability.

Sir: My Norwegian cat Ibsen and I are in love with each other. There is nothing carnal to this lifelong affection, and we already enjoy a very civil union, but we feel we would like to have the relationship given formal divine blessing. Is there any branch of any organized religion which would arrange such a ceremony?

I got the idea of the sanctified furniture from the Ashanti people, who had been venerating their own sacred throne for centuries, but it has not yet caught on in Britain. Similarly, my dear friend Ibsen died in 2016 without our union receiving any sacred blessing, even in Wales.

DAY 69

I don't want to sound curmudgeonly, but I do not approve of literary prizes. It is true that I would not mind winning one, instead of being a habitual runner-up, and I would not say no to being half a century or so younger than I am and thus qualified to win one of those prizes specifically reserved for young writers. No, it is not just envy that animates me; it is the conviction that art, however elementary, cannot be competitive.

How can anyone rate the merit of one book against another, or this talent with that – like comparing beauty itself, or goodness, or evil? Which would win the prize, *Jane Eyre* or *Ulysses*, Flaubert or Mark Twain? Only a god, an angel or perhaps a genius could judge, and not many are around to preside over the Man Booker or the Pulitzer. I suppose there are, though, writers extant around the world who really are competitive, who are out to be better than the others – not in the matter of sales or even reviews, but out of plain competitiveness, like sportsmen.

The success of some athletes and chess players, it is true, is sometimes abetted by the elegance of their performances, but their true purpose is to beat somebody else by the rules of their practice. There are no rules to art, though, nobody is offside, and to my mind nobody should be judged a winner. Not even me.

DAY 70

One of the pleasures of life, when you reach a certain age and are no longer keen on dinners, is one o'clock lunch. We have long made it a practice to eat it out somewhere, at a different place each day, and there are half a dozen local places we frequent, each with a different allure. There is a grand old pub a mile up the road, for instance, where good whitebait is served at the bar, and there is a decorous tea shop downtown (i.e. in Cricieth, population 1,800), where I enjoy presenting agnostic arguments to its gently evangelical owner. The local fishing lakes serve agreeable waterside snacks; we can conveniently park the car at Tesco's while we eat toasted tea cakes at the café across the road. There is an original choice of light lunches at a restaurant in the next town along the coast – so excellent that I have twice been fined for parking too long outside its doors – and the restaurant at our local garden centre seems to me an ideal example of Welsh capitalism.

How many is that? Six? Ah well, the seventh is showier than the rest, so we often skip it, but alas it offers the best lunch of the lot. It is on our local waterfront, with a view of the castle, and the following is my own weekly favourite: a piping hot iron cauldron of local moules marinière, with rough fresh bread, a glass of Sauvignon Blanc and a large cappuccino to conclude.

I sometimes feel like a second cauldron of mussels, showy or not, but no, I restrain myself for another week.

Feeling short of inspiration.
Here's my message to the nation:
If you've nothing much to say,
Put your consciences away.
You need not work to earn a living!
Make Idleness its own Thanksgiving!

See you tomorrow!

DAY 71B

I had a jolt last night. I realized that I am not the me I always was. I know, of course, that in my ninety-second year of a lovely quick life my limbs aren't so lithe as they were, my eyesight is not so keen, my daily exercise has slowed. My handwriting, once proudly bold, has diminished into mingyness, and sometimes my spelling lets me down – even my speech occasionally, when I forget words or splutter.

I accept all this, though, however reluctantly, as the normal concomitant of old age – senility creeping in. But it was something altogether else that gave me that jolt last night. I had just turned down some enticing propositions from my agent – enjoyable public appearances at home and abroad. The circumstances were fine, the money would be very welcome, and I was just about to pick up the telephone and gratefully accept the offer when –

I realized that I was not me any more. It wasn't that I was tired of myself – I would surely have enjoyed those commissions. But I felt I now needed otherness, to inhabit some other, different sphere, to explore some other avenues, to breathe differently perhaps, or think some other way in another kind of existence, in another sort of me.

If you know what I am yearning for, what sphere or what avenue, what me, do let me know. But hurry, please, so I can reassure my family, or let my dear agent know after all.

DAY 72

It is 140 years, I am astonished to realize, since the one true spiritual influence on my life came into this world. The theologian Claude Jenkins was already an eminent canon of Christ Church, Oxford, when I sang there as a child chorister, and so for several years I often received, with the congregation, his evening benediction. The style of it, as he slowly recited it in the gathering dusk before the distant high altar, fascinated me then as it moves me in memory now. So very old he looked up there, so mystical seemed his vestmented figure in the half-light and so lovely did his blessing sound in the words of the King James Bible that he seemed to me a very emblem of simple goodness, beyond all dogma, thesis or even his own theology. The image, like the example, has remained with me ever since.

Years afterwards, he christened, at the same cathedral, my second son, Henry (his godfather was Ed Hillary of Everest), and a friend of mine told me he saw the by then venerable scholar unsuccessfully trying to take the hand of the baby in his crib.

'Insufficiently prehensile,' the dear old boy was allegedly murmuring.

DAY 73

There are many conveniences to twenty-first-century life in the capitalist West, and in most ways it is undoubtedly true that, as the Etonian Harold Macmillan once told us in a politically correct vernacular, we have never had it so good. In other ways, though, we have never had it so bloody awful, and one small contemporary misery concerns packaging.

To my mind there are few more infuriating demands in daily life than the task of getting sugar out of one of those beastly little paper tubes that come with the coffee in most cafés. They are nasty in themselves, and almost impossible to open except by biting their ends off, and when at last I succeed in the task (I have a sweet tooth) I am left with horrid little twists of cheap brown paper, littering my place at the table, for which I can find no polite means of disposal. (Leave them in the saucer? Hide them underneath? Pretend to drop them on the floor by mistake?)

It is bad enough opening the cornflakes packet, or even just getting a volume out of a parcel from an old-school bookseller (your modern online practitioners, however much you may deplore their effect upon tradition, certainly know how to pack a book conveniently).

And then again, gift packaging, sweet though it may be with red ribbons and holly, can be a perfect curse to get into – can it not? – and is surely yet another unnecessary contribution to the developed world's mountain of garbage. One of my favourite scenes in film comedy, from the movie *Love Actually*, has Rowan Atkinson as a department store assistant packing up a gift. What a time he takes! With what infinite delicacy he folds the paper, ornamentally ties the twine, smooths the packaging and at last offers it to the customer with a sublimely ingratiating smirk. He has made of the job, as he might say, a tiny work of art.

But it is destined only to be impatiently torn apart, scrumpled and thrown away, as the heedless recipient scrambles for her booty.

Moral: There is none. Like it or not, we've never had it so good.

DAY 74

Scraped, torn and shabby inside the door of my car are two paperback volumes of Michel de Montaigne's collected essays. They live there permanently, and I love them. I have them at home in two much better hardback editions, but these old friends, shoved rudely but conveniently beside my driving seat, are dearer to me.

This is because to my mind they are the very best antidote to boredom. I do not read them, of course, while I am driving, but the moment I am held up, because of roadworks or traffic lights, because I am waiting to meet somebody's train or because I've dropped Elizabeth off at the hairdressers, the moment I switch my engine off – ha! – I scrabble happily for my Montaigne. The two old volumes, which I have had almost as long as the car itself, were one volume once, but I tore it into two halves to get them into the door pocket, and since they are a very tight fit still, poor things, they have a sort of brave, uncomplaining look to them that I find extra endearing.

Of course, they might be made for dipping into. Was there ever another writer anywhere more instantly readable and friendly? What do I feel like reading about while I wait? Liars? Idleness? Pedantry? The Power of the Imagination? The Custom of Wearing Clothes? Names? War Horses? The Education of Children? Anger? Cowardice? The Disadvantage of Greatness?

All these, and a hundred more, are waiting there for my contemplation, but better still, Michel is waiting there too, and there was never a kinder, cleverer and more beguiling companion to share ideas with, while the old Honda gratefully takes a breather.

Wales is rarely associated with commercial capitalism, but the names of several great London stores remember the enterprise of expatriate money-makers long ago, and when Welsh people go in for it on their home ground the result can be admirable. This is because they often manage to make it at once homely, efficient and profitable.

Take an example up the road from us. Twenty years ago a farming family there decided to extend their property and exploit their inherited skills by starting a garden centre. This is now a complex of five or six large greenhouses surrounded by flowerbeds, equipped with all modern devices and chock-a-block full of every garden plant under the sun. At Christmas the centre becomes in part a delightfully illuminated sort of grotto.

It is much more than that, though. A generation later, the family added to the complex an agreeable small restaurant, and this has turned the whole project into a very cheerful sort of institution. The key to its success is a homely Welsh kind of sophistication. Staff or customers, nearly everyone in the place seems to know somebody else. Multitudinous children whizz about in search of ice creams, fondly supervised by proud mums and lenient, talkative dads. Familiar members of the farm family attend the counters or serve the tables, helpings are generous, a bookstall in one corner offers a cornucopia of paperbacks about Wales, and the Welsh language predominates.

That's the way to do it! I don't know, of course, how much money it makes. I always feel it gives as much pleasure to its owners as it does to its customers, but then I suppose that's the nature of capitalism – at least when the employees, the third party so to speak, are all in the family, all at home, and all Welsh too.

DAY 76

This Diary of Thoughts deliberately does not concern itself with world affairs, politics or ideologies, but aims (if it has an aim) simply to record my personal meditations, datelessly.

Today it has a date – 31 January 2017 – because it marks the end of the first tumultuous week of the American presidency of Donald Trump, and I feel the need to record my own responses to his eruption into all our consciousnesses. What do I think of him this morning?

The look of him I detest, and the voice, and the crude vocabulary, and the bigotries, and the headlong, show-off decisions.

The style of him I rather admire, because it is basically apolitical. He throws himself into those decisions as though he alone has the power of authority, without the trammels of the constitution or the complexities of legality, showing the brash, all-American filmic confidence, party politics apparently disregarded, that obviously won him his election.

Do I trust him? No.

But in the long run, will he be a successful president? I rather think he may. Think of the grasping Saul: a single vision on the road to Damascus improbably made a saint of him, and perhaps this brash plutocrat, this showy TV star, this Trump Towers exhibitionist with the golden elevator will meet the angels of his own better self during the four years of his presidential journey.

Do I really think that?

I don't know. Tomorrow is another dateless day.

I am big on premonitions. Sometimes they prove true, sometimes not. Nearly twenty years ago I returned from a world journey feeling that something dire was about to happen to the world. The very next day, the World Trade Center in New York was attacked by terrorists, and we entered a new zeitgeist.

It is not just a new spirit of the age that I sense is brewing now; it is a fundamental revision of all the ages, and we are witnessing now its very first elementary stirrings. A few days back, I recorded in this diary an infinitely vague, imprecise but nagging feeling that I must myself enter some altogether new kind of existence, and perhaps that was premonitory? Certainly, it seems to me that during all our lifetimes, and reaching a climax now, mankind has been unconsciously preparing itself for some immense renewal – in the elimination of sexual differences, for example, in the gradual abolition of the Nation-State, in the new command of cyberspace and, above all, in the terrific revolution that is artificial intelligence, our own fateful step towards Creation. These are portents more drastic by far than mere suggestions of a new zeitgeist – as the Industrial Revolution was, say, or the World Trade Center tragedy, or going to the moon. And what does my premonition suggest to me about these colossal developments? Only this, ignorant agnostic that I am: that surely, surely, there must be some almighty Power, some Soul (immortal, invisible, God only wise, as the Christian hymn has it) with a vast eternal Plan (as Tevye suggests in *Fiddler on the Roof*); and that the final zeitgeist of all zeitgeists will then be unveiled for us, if ever we can master its meaning.

Until then, Keep Smiling, friend – 'Immortal, Invisible, God Only Knows'.

DAY 78

If he had plenty of money, wrote the poet Browning, he would choose to live in a house in a city square. 'Ah,' said he, 'such a life, such a life, as one leads at the window there!'

I half agree with him. From our windows, front and back, we can only expect to see trees, birds and sheep, plus the occasional car or tractor, and I would not have it otherwise. It is undeniable, though, that one of my great pleasures is to have coffee with my Elizabeth in a particular window seat of a café in Porthmadog and watch our small world go by. The window looks out directly at a pedestrian crossing, so that every few minutes the passing traffic is going to stop for a moment, and a cluster of people assemble at the pavement's edge, waiting for the lights to change. So I have a chance to assess our version of the life out there.

Some of it, of course, consists of our own neighbours, and we are able to observe that Mrs S looks particularly spritely that morning, or that old W obviously got out of the wrong side of his bed . . . More often they are strangers, and then we are able to conjecture. 'Happy in marriage, don't you think?' 'Just getting over a tiff?' 'What a bore, to have to lead that poor dog everywhere on a lead.' 'Goodness, the grocery bag should keep them going, and they're plump enough already.' 'That old dear will have to hurry if she wants to get across before the lights change. Oh no, good, it's OK, that nice-looking youth is going to help her – surely he's the Ws' boy, isn't he? What an excellent family they are, except perhaps for . . .'

But hang about. A small climax arises. Few of those people notice us noticing them, but here is a covey of four or five small children, with two determined women, in and around a perambulator. When the light changes and they step off the pavement to cross the street, the children one and all look up at our window, straight in the eye at us. We wave at them, and then our little world erupts in merriment. Violently they wave back, one and all, laughing and making funny faces at us, while their harassed mothers gamely continue their passage across the street, sometimes pausing to pick up a dropped glove or teddy bear and offering us wry sisterly laughs too.

And so they pass out of our sight, the lights change again and the traffic resumes. We finish our coffee and, laughing too, pack up our own purchases to go home. 'Ah,' we say to ourselves, 'what a slice of life it was, what a lively little corner of the world, that we saw at the window there!'

DAY 79

I have been in tremulous, transcendent mood during the last few days, searching in my mind for some denouement, I know not what. The very world seems so uncertain of itself, mired in discord great and petty, short of conviction or objective, lurching from headline to headline, rumorous, squabbling and variously timid and arrogant. Is some Second Coming coming? Where should I look? What should I hope for? Is there a God after all?

Into this mental quagmire there has fallen a new edition of Wordsworth's immense poem *The Prelude*, with a commission to review it for a magazine. During the past few days, I have reread the whole of this work, often aloud, and I have ended, if not restored or reassured about the state of the world, at least enchanted by the magic of the verse – partly, of course, by the music of it, the lilts and the rhythms, but chiefly by what I take to be its own moral conclusion, namely that existence itself, as expressed in its simplest and kindest natural forms, is the ultimate meaning of life, and our own grandest recompense.

Wordsworth, bless his heart, seemed to conclude that if there is a God, Nature is the breath of it, and Art its language. If so, then one of the divine messengers must surely be the Poet, even when he writes in blank verse, and in three hundred pages of iambic pentameter.

DAY 80

We lost our heroic Norwegian cat Ibsen some time ago, and it really was like saying goodbye to an old and trusted friend. When, among the ornaments in a gardening shop the other day, we saw a lifelike cat replica, we immediately bought it as a sort of stand-in.

It is really not in the least like Ibsen, but it is quite astonishingly like a cat. It is made of concrete, I am told, probably in China, reconstructed by some miraculous photographic technique and now for ever sleeping snugly in a corner of our sofa. I cannot get out of my mind the illusion that it really is alive, and still often reach down to stroke it or murmur comradely endearments. It reminds me of some little couplets I wrote years ago in tribute not to a particular cat, but to the idea of a cat, cat in the abstract. So here they are, as they appeared in Richard Adams's anthology *Occasional Poets* (1986):

Move over, says the Cat, nine-tenths of the bed are
mine.
Yes, in lives and comfort, the ratio's one to nine.

My Cat is Sleep made flesh and fur:
Is death itself a Purr?

Oh, oh, the crime of the claw, the Kraken eye!

It is only a game: may the best mouse die.

I watch through all th'Eternity of the Soul,
In case – in case – ah, Ecstasy – the heap gives forth
A Mole.

DAY 81

'You are about to close two tabs,' my computer has just warned me. 'Are you sure you want to continue?' It often says things like this. Sometimes it informs me that something I am writing is for reading only, and sometimes it lets me know that I am about to close a further four tabs. I have no idea what it's all about. What is a tab, and what is going to happen if I lose one?

It is sad to admit it, I suppose, but I am more or less cyber-illiterate. Children an eighth of my age understand the lingo better than I do, and are very nice about it too, and never laugh at my incompetence or resent having to put me straight. 'Do you see that red button at the top right of the screen? Well, press that and at the same time keep the hold button down – no, the hold button, the one next to it – that's it – now press Shift, and there you are! You see? Nothing to it! Any time!'

I very much like this sharing of skills between the generations, in my experience so kindly demonstrated, and wonder if it could foretell some profounder distribution of human responsibilities? More power to Youth? Less authority for Maturity? I can't imagine how, but then the young are better at imagining things than I am . . .

DAY 82

Most small towns in the islands of Britain have ancient origins, and generally display the evidence. Ancient churches abound. Sometimes there is a castle to see, or an old manor house, and there is sure to be a local historian around to tell you all about it.

Cricieth (*sic* – it's Welsh), our little town on Cardigan Bay in north-west Wales, is no exception. It has an ancient ruined castle on a seafront promontory and a storied history of war and seafaring, and since I have lived nearby for seventy years you might suppose it could offer me nothing new. Every now and then, though, I come across some aspect of the little town, some grace note, that gives me a new sense of intimacy, and today, walking off a vinous lunch, I came across such a suggestive detail. I cannot claim grace for it, because it was really hardly more than a rubbishy backyard, but it still seemed to me wonderfully evocative of the town's storied past.

Cricieth was transformed in the nineteenth century by the arrival of the railway from England, which transformed it into a tourist destination and buried much of it in Victorian and later reconstructions. Here and there medieval cottages remain, lovingly restored, but what I came across today was a shabby and neglected patch of scrubland, in the heart of the town, which generations of developers seem to have overlooked. I stood there transfixed in the afternoon silence, because it seemed to me that I had strayed into the Middle Ages. The old cans and broken bottles that lay about had surely been left there by roistering herring fishermen, or been thrown out, I thought, by skivvies from the castle up the hill. The broken-down sheds had been commandeered, I imagined, by the besieging soldiers of Owain Glyndŵr himself, and perhaps some of the odd bric-a-brac lying around was memorial to their gusto.

Nobody broke the spell for me. There was no noise. The breeze that blew the rubbish about seemed to me authentically medieval, and it was only when I left the place, and found the level crossing gates open to let the two carriages of the 2.30 for Porthmadog chug through, that I decided I would have another cappuccino after all.

DAY 83

I am feline by instinct, and in general I'm not awfully fond of dogs. I don't like the smell of them, I hate being licked by them, I resent being barked at, bitten by or scared by them, and I despise them for their slavish acceptance of domestic mastery. However, there are times when I am almost sentimentally reconciled to the creatures, and yesterday was one of them.

It was a fine brisk sunny morning when I went for my exercise along the promenade, and the whole beach was alive with Dogs. They were of all sorts and breeds, big and small, and freed for once of their leads they not only scampered all over the pebbles, chasing things, but actually rushed frenziedly into the incoming tide-waves, emerging only to shake salt water all over their owners and sending children screaming out of range.

As I leant on the railing above watching the scene, I thought what a bore it must be to have to take those animals out for exercise each morning, to feed them and clear up their excrement and brush their wretched bristles off the sofa and get somebody to look after them when I wanted an evening to myself. What a world away, I thought, from the civilization of the Cats! But no. The more I watched the scene, the more I looked at the faces around and below me, human and canine too, the more I realized that a genuine spirit of affection, and even gratitude, linked the species

146

there. The children loved being splashed, and the dogs loved splashing them. The grown-ups felt young again as they retreated laughing from the spray, and laughed up at me too, to share the fun.

And on the promenade beside me, I realized, were many solitary elderly people, with terriers and lapdogs at their feet, who were watching the goings-on with genuine affection, with pride and with gratitude. I saw then that they wouldn't in the least mind clearing up the shit, or sending the eiderdown to the cleaners again, or taking darling Pongo out for his exercise in the drizzle, or arranging yet again for an evening dog-sitter. I realized that I was witnessing an unwitting reconciliation of species, a shared celebration and a declaration of understanding.

I went home thoughtfully then, remembering my late great love, our Norwegian Forest cat Ibsen, and wondering how happily, if push had come to shove, I would have taken him down to the beach on a lead to entertain the children and demonstrate our comity. I would have despaired. He would have hissed or pissed. Or both.

DAY 84

When I walk my daily thousand paces of exercise I generally do it in military style, which is to say that I march in the manner I learnt during my time in the British Army seventy-odd years ago. It was not at all a swaggering style, more stately if anything, arms swinging to shoulder level, head held high, eyes to the front. The parade pace was dignified and confident; the purpose, I assume, was grandeur.

I have noticed lately, though, that my marching style has changed. It's not so stiff as it used to be, not so formal. I march more in the old American way now, more relaxed, bending my arms at the elbow, and even looking amiably around me. What would the old drill sergeants say?!

It is true that the armed forces of the deceased British Empire, now parading under very different flags, and to different ideologies, still sometimes march in a recognizably British manner, but generally I can hardly recognize my old Aldershot, Catterick or Sandhurst purposes in the military manner of today; and to pull myself together as I stride, I often find myself humming or whistling, to an imaginary symphony orchestra, Elgar's marvellous tune 'Land of Hope and Glory'.

'Dear God,' I hear you exclaim. 'That old bombast! Make us Mightier yet!' Yes, because whatever the idiot jingoists do with the melody at the Promenade Concerts, clownishly jumping up and down to its rhythms, I believe

this hymn nobly expresses grander values than mere patriotism. I prefer to think of its tremendous theme, whatever
Elgar thought of it himself, not as bombast or plain swank,
but as an anthem boasting of the heroic survival down the
ages, in triumph as in tribulation, of all of us, all mankind
together.

So as I come to the end of my walk, when I hear the
ghostly command of the regimental sergeant-major order-
ing me to pull myself together, get my head up and pull my
shoulders back, I gratefully do what I am told.

Like it or not, I remind myself, we are still on parade!

DAY 85

I am stunned, simply stunned, by the amount of stuff that is packed inside my perfectly ordinary brain. It is true that nowadays the mechanism isn't working as well as it used to. I forget names now, and where I put things, and what the day is, and how to spell 'rheumatism', and even sometimes how to speak words. Nevertheless, looking up something now in the *Oxford Dictionary of Quotations*, I am astonished to realize how much of its contents – 1,075 pages of it – is stored in my mind already, with all its associations, and how it can be accessed by a simple trigger. For example, put in the words 'lone and level', and instantly up comes in my memory Ozymandias. 'Smokestack'? Of course, I see in my mind's eye a dirty British coaster. 'Merrily, merrily shall I live now,' and there is that sprite of the island celebrating his release. 'Men will still say,' and we can almost hear the drone of the bombers.

You know what I mean, I'm sure: somewhere in our skulls an entire encyclopedia is stored, only awaiting an index. And if you are musical, even more phenomenal is your brain's command of melody. My brother Gareth, a professional musician, could infallibly identify for me from a single phrase, even a single note, what classical work it came from, and I am astonished to discover myself, from the quotations book, how readily I can summon an old tune from its first line or its title. Try it yourself!

'A Couple of Swells'? 'Fish gotta swim, Birds gotta fly'? 'Hallelujah!' 'Over There!' 'All Through the Night'.

'Arrival of the Queen of Sheba'.

There you are – if you're anything like me you're whistling already!

It's all up there in the mind, all the time, or alternatively, in the *Oxford Dictionary of Quotations*.

DAY 86

I have spent a happy few hours contemplating the work of the Welsh artist Thomas Jones (1742–1803). Do you know about him? He was a Radnorshire country gentleman who became in his youth a skilful disciple of Richard Wilson, the founder of British landscape painting, and spent some years in Italy cultivating his gifts. His pictures were generally admired: after his death they commanded good prices and were hung in galleries all over the place. His was never one of your household names, though, even among the cognoscenti, and he was never as celebrated as his master, until in 1954 there came to light a very small painting of his, a few inches square, that made him a celebrity in the art world.

It dated from his Italian days, it was called simply *A Wall in Naples*, and that was about it. It seemed to picture the blank and slightly crumbled wall of a perfectly ordinary old Italian townhouse, with three windows in a row, the left-hand one in good shape, the middle one with a balcony and a line of washing, the right-hand one apparently disused, or never completed and bricked up. The composition seemed so totally out of period, though, in style and in matter, that it was hailed as a first example of Modern Art, abstract art perhaps, containing subtle suggestions and messages. Some critics thought it really meant nothing at all. One declared it to be 'the very stuff of illusion', and to others the picture was some secretive kind of alle-gory, or evidence of the artist's own habitual melancholy. There was something haunting about it.

The latest scholarly interpreter has been Mr Michael Tomlinson, who has written a brilliant long essay about the picture. It was published in the *Transactions of the Honourable Society of Cymmrodorion*, and it has drastic-ally affected my own responses to *A Wall in Naples*. For myself, I have long thought the picture might represent the Three Ages of Man, thus: window 1 – confident youth; window 2 (the one with the washing) – domesticized mid-dle age; window three – elderly dereliction. Tomlinson, though, has taught me otherwise. He has convinced me that the picture has a solemn religious meaning, and is directly descended from the Passion scenes of the medi-eval Italian masters. The three windows are the three crosses of Calvary (the complete ones have cruciform shutter closures), and the strip of linen hanging from the central one identifies it, if you look at it in the right frame of mind, as the Lord's own. Moreover, if you concentrate your attention, just to the left of that balcony do you not see signs that some liquid has been sloshed down the wall there – not poured, as you might expect, from the front of the balcony, away from the masonry, but at one side of it?

What is that, Mr Tomlinson surmises, but Jones's own reminder to us of the blood and water that flowed from Jesus's side, pierced by the soldier's spear and immortal-ized by generations of earlier artists. This reverent new interpretation has clinched for me the enigma of *A Wall in Naples*, and convinced me of its profounder genius. 'Far from being about nothing,' says Mr Tomlinson, 'it is about everything.'

Only one nagging surmise remains in my own mind. What if Thomas Jones, surveying his own rather barren townscape picture, decided to make an allegory of it after all, and added all the holy hints? Anyway, *A Wall in Naples* now hangs in the National Gallery in London, and is haunting still.

DAY 87

That's odd. I don't seem to have thought anything today. It does happen.

DAY 88

I've been reading about an Anglican bishop, somewhere in England, who adamantly won't recognize the right of women to be priests. Although there are many women priests in his own diocese, he says he certainly wouldn't accept Holy Communion, the ultimate sacrament of his beliefs, from one of them. In fact, he wouldn't even accept Communion from a male priest who had been ordained by a woman, and he belongs to a society of clergy supplied with cards that trace their own ordinations back to ordinations by predecessors who were themselves, thank the Lord, NOT FEMALE!!!

As a fairly muzzy agnostic myself, I certainly do not expect rationality in religion – anything but! – but I really do think this takes nuttiness too far, rivalling any of those medieval absurdities about angels dancing on pinheads. And I certainly cannot understand why Christians demand anything more of their faith than what they get from the teaching of Jesus – embodied, just to make it easy for them, in the marvellous semi-fable of his life. They needn't believe all the stuff about miracles, etc.; just observe what he does and says himself – 'Go, and do thou likewise!'

Old-school mumbo-jumbo may be dead and gone, but magic of a far profounder kind lives on in philosophy and art. All the great religions, I suspect, absorb those

marvellous imponderables somewhere in their often con-
fusing creeds, and good people everywhere, ordained or
not, go forth and do likewise . . .

DAY 89

I have always been fond of the Anglo-French word 'louche', though I have not always translated it correctly. I used it admiringly in writing an obituary, years ago, of my friend and colleague Ralph Izzard, and his widow gently rebuked me for it. It is true that the *Oxford English Dictionary* says 'louche' implies 'sordid in a rakish or appealing way'. I rather hazily think of it, though, as being elegantly urbane, experienced, ironical and fun, and that's how I think of Ralph still . . . I think of cities that way too. In particular, I cherish the memory of Manhattan before the rot set in, and just occasionally wish I could still be there, in a small sophisticated bar somewhere, dim-lit, with love around and soft musicianly jazz on a white piano. So 'OK,' said I to my own love early last night, 'let's go downtown and get ourselves a martini.'

The joint we went to was not dim-lit, somewhere on the Upper West Side. No yellow cabs went by. No piano played, and I had known the waitress's family for years. But the sun was setting over the bay outside, lights were flickering in our little Welsh town, love was in the air and I felt proper louche.

DAY 90

I've been thinking a lot about walls, having lately spent some hours contemplating a particularly enigmatic example of the genre in an eighteenth-century painting, and it occurs to me that The Wall, in capital letters, is one of the dominant symbols of the human condition (together, perhaps, with its unassuming alter ego, the ditch). I don't know if the Garden of Eden was walled, but down the centuries many thousands of humans have accepted that God himself is ever present in the Wailing Wall at Jerusalem.

And from that supreme destiny, think of all the other walls that have lodged themselves into our languages and our psyches: Hadrian's Wall, the Aurelian Wall, the Great Wall of China, the Berlin Wall, Offa's Dyke, Thisbe's Wall, Trump's Wall, the stone walls that don't a prison make, the monstrous concrete wall that damned developer's putting up . . . It is not, on the whole, an agreeable aura – is it? – that attends the idea of The Wall. To be sure, the construction is often protective, but it is far more often alienating, and it is not generally kindly of numen or appearance.

Sometimes, though, walls do strike me as intriguingly arcane, and fortunately for me, a few examples of that hazy allure wind their lonely dry-stone way over the mountains behind my home. Just what they are for, I know not. Once, no doubt, they formed a boundary of some sort, or even a frontier, as they did in many such landscapes of the Celtic north. Perhaps they still serve some such purpose, concerned with grazing rights or tithe collection. Mostly, though, I prefer to think, they are meaningless, purpose-less, suggestive, understood only by themselves and the wandering sheep – unless, of course, they are all subsid-iary accommodations of the Wailing Wall . . .

Our modest and crumbling house, Trefan Morys, is just about as old as the United States of America, but has this to be said for it: it has its fill of curiosities. Here are some of them – stand back! Scores of model ships, of many kinds, materials and nationalities, are scattered through its rooms, and they include a large steamship flying the fated flag of the Free City of Danzig (1920–39), and the green-grocer's barge from which we used to buy our groceries when we lived in Venice, and a wooden New York tug built (it says on the bottom) by Colonel Willsey Dubois, and an Arab dhow, and a Faroe Islands fishing boat, and a Bristol Channel pilot boat . . .

Then again, framed in our library is a bit of the metal pipe through which was watered the original Morgan horse, in Vermont, at the end of the eighteenth century, and framed close by is a manuscript of the poem 'The Country Clergy', written for me in his own hand by the greatest of modern Welsh poets, R. S. Thomas (died 2000). That iron trident was used long ago by predecessors in the house to spear salmon in our river, and under a carpet, to keep it flat, is a glorious *Atlas of Egypt*, published in 1928 and dedicated to His Majesty King Farouk. On the somewhat ramshackle little terrace outside is a bronze bust, which I commissioned from an eminent New Zealand sculptor, of Admiral of the Fleet Lord Fisher of Kilverstone, who died in 1920, and with whom I propose to have an affair in the afterlife.

'Enough, enough,' do I hear you grumble? 'Give us a rest!' Well, there's more to come, and who's in charge here, anyway?

As I warned you yesterday, here are some more eccentri-
cities of our home in Wales. Scattered through it are some
thirty architectural models and toys, of buildings ranging
from the house itself by way of the Leaning Tower of Pisa,
Caernarfon Castle, the Burj Al Arab at Dubai, the Royal
Crescent at Bath, the Radcliffe Camera, a Thai stilt-house
and an inn in Wyoming. Then again, that framed letter
over there is a farewell note from a reader who was about
to enter a closed-order convent, the big photograph in the
kitchen of the liner *Queen Elizabeth* entering New York I
keep because its publishers got the name of the ship wrong,
while in the bathroom that enormous coloured print of the
SS *New York* also entering the city was presented, I am
told, to every first-class passenger on the vessel's maiden
voyage in 1888.

The peculiar bright paintings on the landing were pre-
liminary cartoons for some mighty imperial panels painted
by Frank Brangwyn in 1930 for the House of Lords; the
project was rejected by their lordships, and the panels
themselves now adorn Swansea City Hall. The cartoons
are bright and breezy.

All five members of my immediate family are represented by miscellaneous works of art, strewn through the
house from one end to the other, and under the stairs a
slate dutifully awaits the departure of Jan and Elizabeth

Morris, 'at the end of one life', when it will be placed with happy ceremonial, I hope, on an islet we possess in the nearby River Dwyfor.

And finally, several million books are embedded and entangled, as it were, in the very character, psyche and ethos of Trefan Morys. I have read them all, and written most of them.

There you go! Keep Smiling!

DAY 93

'Chaos', the dictionary tells me, is a state of complete confusion and disorder, such as existed before the cosmos was created. I know it well, and I know that, whatever the ancients thought, it is a perpetually renewable condition. It grows more completely frightful, in fact, as civilization progresses, at least as it can be estimated by the condition of desks. Just think how ordered our forebears' work desks must have been, before electronics arrived, let alone cybernetics. The steam age presumably made little difference to Great-Grandfather's working conditions: a notebook or two, a pen rack, a bottle of ink and blotting paper, a simple address book, some writing paper and a pen, and he was perfectly equipped for senior management of the workhouse, or at least for family authority. But look at your own desk – or more pertinently, look at mine. To an almost legendary, pre-biblical degree, Chaos is here. Beneath my feet there is a sinuous confusion of wires, twisting and coiling down there as though they are about to squirm up and throttle me. They may even be hissing. Other tentacles come wriggling out of nowhere among the miscellaneous computers, telephones, iPads, printers, discarded mechanisms and scrumpled packets of wine gums that litter my workspace above.

And yet, and yet . . . I do not resent this minor maelstrom. That song about old familiar places – remember it? – comes into my mind as I untangle myself from those electronic coils, hazily work out the right thing to click, optimistically ignore the blue light blinking on that black box over there and invite into the morning old friend Google. Oh good, there's one wine gum left. Contentedly humming that tune about familiar places, I start work on my ninety-fourth Thought . . .

DAY 94

One of the most marvellous inventions of the time, it seems to me, is sight recognition. You know, devices that automatically know the look of you, unlock your car or authorize your passport. Wouldn't it be wonderful if it could be made to remember names for you at moments of need – match them, that is, against faces that you have known for years and years, but can't at that moment for the life of you identify?

The infuriating thing is that it is actually in your possession. At the moment the old acquaintance reaches out his hand to you, clear as daylight his name is shining or blinking somewhere inside your brain. You know it perfectly well, but you just can't get hold of it in there. What a miracle it would be if in a flash your Photo Recognizer would send a requirement to your Face Register, instantly find a match and transfer it to your Consciousness!

'Fancy recognizing me after all these years!' good old What's-'Is-Name would exclaim in astonishment. 'My wife will be impressed.'

'Oh,' you would affectionately reply, 'I never forget a face. Never forget a name, for that matter. How is dear Audrey, by the way?'

DAY 95

I can still hear myself, when I think about it, replying to an American lady in Cairo who asked me if I was British. It was sometime in the late 1940s, I would guess, and being British in Egypt then was not always comfortable. 'Say, are you British?' she wanted to know, and I answered in kind.

'O, *very* British,' said I.

What another world it was in those days! To be British then meant something altogether different – to her, to the world at large and to me. But it would not last. Americans would soon begin to lose the inherited respect that so many of them felt towards the Old Country. The nations of the Second World War would presently forget Churchill's heroic Britain, of the cockneys and the Spitfires. The British Empire was no more, and people would not so often think of themselves as utterly British at all.

And by now, as the very conception of Britain, let alone Great Britain (GB), seems to be fading, and the so-called United Kingdom (UK) is apparently disintegrating, people like me look back with irony to our old certainties. Actually, though, it was never really Britain I felt emotional about. Mine was too complex a loyalty to explain to the American in Cairo that day, but it was by no means a country-right-or-wrong sort of pride. It was pride in an abstraction, and its name was not Britain, but England.

It is subsumed nowadays in my love for Wales and Welshness, but still in my heart I always hear, as poets have down the generations, the English siren call. The gentle beauty of England's countryside was part of it, and the grandeur of its history, and the humour that ran through its affairs, and the melancholy, and the ironic blend of right and wrong, and Shakespeare, and what people like me always fondly thought of as an essential kindliness.

But never fear! The UK seems to be disintegrating around us, GB is losing its meaning, but no doubt that old dream of England will lyrically survive the debacle.

DAY 96

'I am dying, Egypt, dying,' observed Antony to Cleopatra, and actually it went without saying. We all are. The fact is starker, though, when you reach my status in life.

My mathematics never were reliable, but I worked out this morning that I have so far been in this world for 375,000 days! Is that possible? Is that conceivable? Is that how you spell 'conceivable'?

If that's the truth, it dawns upon me that I face an urgent task, comparable in kind to the British withdrawal from Europe – my Morrexit from life. I am totally ill equipped for it. Have I made a will? Where is it? Who am I leaving things to?

What is an Executor? What is a Literary Executor?

Who arranges a funeral? Who pays for it? Who tells Authority that I have gone?

Oh, it's all a mystery to me, like preferential tariff concessions within or without pre-compensatory European agreements, and I greatly envy old Antony, who simply informed his love poetically and kicked the bucket.

DAY 97

In nostalgic mood, at random a week or two ago I picked up a city book of my own to read in the bath, and so embarked upon a recollection of all my twenty-odd books concerning cities around the world.

The piece I read in the tub concerned the Canadian city of Saskatoon, Saskatchewan, and I wrote it in 1990. I had hardly been there before, and as I turned the dripping pages of the volume I realized with a jolt what gross effrontery it had been, all my life, to barge uninvited and ignorant into such a city and write a totally uninhibited critique about its character! Uninformed! Uninvited! What insolence!

And then, in chastened introspection, it occurred to me that all my work about cities really had been one long bit of cheek. I hardly knew what I was writing about in all those cities. I did nearly everything, as musicians would say, by ear, making it up as I went along. Serious historians and geographers must have despised my intentions and techniques; sociologists must have thought me flippant; scholars found lots of errors (I never could differentiate longitude from latitude).

But there we are. Even Saskatooners must admit I got something right – I liked the place! A genuinely characterful city, I called it. They should see what I wrote about Sydney, in my callow days . . .

DAY 98

A distinguished Arab diplomat brought his wife to visit us yesterday. I never enjoyed a visit more. I was at my most self-centred and complacent; they were most charmingly indulgent. So cosmopolitan was their bearing that only gradually did I recognize in my own responses a spell out of my distant past, a particular kind of charm that powerfully affected my youth: the spell of the Arabs.

What was it exactly? It was partly the beauty of Islam, particularly as it was expressed in its splendid architecture, but also in what I admired about its faith. It was partly the Arabic language, which I briefly and inadequately studied. It was the romance of the Arab landscapes, and the grand sweep of Arab history, and the dust and desert and legend of it all.

Chiefly, though, it was the pleasure of the people – the Arab colleagues I worked with, the Arab neighbours I shared, the Arabs of all kinds I wrote about.

It's many long years since my stay in the Arab countries ended, and since then the reputation of the Arabs and their noble religion has been coarsened, cheapened and betrayed. Our visitors yesterday reminded me again of the fascination that so bewitched me long ago.

Exercising with T. S. Eliot

If I set out in the morning for my statutory thousand daily paces up the lane, very likely whistling a cocky melody, my friendly exact shadow precedes me on the ground and encourages me to assess myself – my shadow at morning, as *The Waste Land* has it, striding before me!

In some ways I like myself well enough then. I enjoy the fun of me, the harmless conceit, the guileless complexity and the merriment. When I go walking in the evening, on the other hand, my shadow is less distinct and less encouraging, rising blurred to reproach me as the sun fades. I shall not be whistling then, but humming some more thoughtful theme, and I shall recognize what I don't like about myself – selfishness, self-satisfaction, foolish self-deceit and irritability.

Morning pride, then, and evening shame. But so what? Either way, I think the poet tells me, no more than a handful of dust . . .

Ill Temper

Oh, it would be nice on this, my centenary diary day, to contribute some kindly thought. The morning is fine outside my window. A dozen lambs are messing around down there, intermittently breaking off for a suck at their patient mums or a combined attempt to get through a hole in the gate. Somebody has just gone merrily past on a quad bike, and on the face of it you may think it sounds all for the best in the best of all possible worlds.

It is not.

It is most certainly not.

For the fifth day running the garage man has not, as promised, returned my car after its servicing.

Has he not lent me a car in its stead?

He has, and a ghastly old thing it is, obliging me ignominiously to inquire of him how I could make it go backwards.

Have I an urgent need to use it?

Well, no, but that's not the point.

What's wrong with it?

Nothing in particular. I just don't like it.

Do you like the garage man?

He's all right.

You like him?

Well, yes, I do actually.

Well, then, what's the matter?

Those lambs are driving me crazy, that's what, and when is that person going to stop driving up and down the lane, that's what, and it's five whole days, going on six, since the garage man promised my car would be back with me, that's chiefly what.

Anything more you want to know, Nosey Parker? No? You thought I was going to end this centenary thought with some gentle, kindly quip, didn't you?

WELL, YOU'RE BLOODY WELL WRONG.

DAY 101

Alas, I'm growing out of touch with Manhattan, one of my favourite places on earth, but from time to time faithful friends report to me about curious goings-on there. To one recent event I here make my own contribution.

It concerns the statue of a bull, eleven feet tall, which stands at a traffic junction in lower Manhattan, in the heart of the Financial District, and was erected in 1989 to celebrate Wall Street's recent recovery from a stock market crash. The Italian-born sculptor Arturo Di Modica made it, and he declared it a symbol of revived prosperity and strength – of American bullishness, in fact!

However, not long ago a rival bronze appeared, altogether unofficially, on the same plinth. It was only four feet tall, and depicted a small pigtailed girl in a wind-blown skirt facing up to the bull. It had been placed there by supporters of women's rights, and to the dismay of Mr Di Modica gave to the sculpture group an altogether different symbolism. Now it became known as the *Fearless Girl* facing the *Charging Bull*, and was generally assumed to honour indomitable Womanhood challenging Male Supremacy.

The response was overwhelmingly favourable. The little bronze girl was given temporary civic permission to stay there, but I hear there is controversy about her permanent future. One of my Manhattan contacts has asked me what I think about it, and what name I would give the group if it were to remain permanently there among the money-makers.

Well now, thought I this morning. *Fearless Girl and Charging Bull* is hardly apt. The child certainly seems dauntlessly cocky, but the bull actually looks rather geriatric, and the whole ensemble suggests to me not a challenge at all, but a fond great-uncle having fun and games in the garden with his patiently obliging little niece. Here, then, is my suggestion for a permanent title:

Playtime in Wall Street.

DAY 102

I have always felt an affinity with the little armadillo known variously as the woodlouse or the doodlebug (a nickname it shared with the wartime German flying bomb, the original cruise missile). I admired the little creature's roly-poly powers, when I was a child, and had my own name for it – the dabblyjoo. Of course, I know now what an infestuous curse it can be, especially in a house like ours with lots of wood in it, and I have learnt that most varieties of woodlice cannot in fact roll themselves into a ball. Never mind, my dabblyjoos certainly could.

This morning, when I went to run my bath there was a woodlouse waiting for me. As the woodlouse custom is, it had doubtless climbed the incoming water pipe, and as my custom is, I prepared to push it safely down again, with a little dribble of water to ease its passage.

Alas, I could not budge it. It didn't exactly make a ball of itself, but it squashed itself flat on the bath's bottom, and disregarding all my fond entreaties, obliged me to scrape it off and send it back down the pipe, with a powerful squirt of water to hasten the process. In short, I murdered it.

'Oh, I am so very sorry,' I said aloud to it, 'that's the very last thing I wanted to do to an old friend, a lifelong colleague and compatriot. Do please forgive me.'

But no, there came no reply, not even a gurgle, from that implacable dabblyjoo. Nature's not what it used to be . . .

178

DAY 103

Today it's all Irony, an abstraction that has long enthralled me with its amalgam of humour, tragedy, cynicism, mystery and surprise. In fact, I've written a short book about it, concerning the Japanese battleship *Yamato*, the most powerful of her day. Beautiful but lethal, she went to her end in the Second World War heroically but unnecessarily, efficiently but ineffectively, stylishly in a squalid cause – ironically, in fact. And all around me this morning, it seems to me, an almighty, universal irony is in performance.

On the one hand, outside my window is happening the loveliest, richest, happiest springtime I can remember. Green, green young Easter leaves are everywhere, late snowdrops jostle early bluebells, impertinent daisies crop up, crocuses lurk among primroses and everywhere birds are enthusiastically nesting. Over the way, yesterday's lambs are lambs no more, but strenuous young sheep showily ignoring their mothers, and all in all this morning the world seems to be halfway to heaven.

It is not. The world is halfway to hell.

Consider the situation out there, beyond the garden, beyond the field with the gambolling young sheep. The unpredictable leader of one State has lately dropped upon another the largest bomb ever dropped anywhere in the history of the world, the loony leader of another is furiously developing nuclear bombs and firing rockets into oceans, the implacable leader of a third has lately been killing opponents with chemical poisons, a fourth is scaring all his neighbours stiff with the possibility of invading them, and through all the arteries of the earth there pulses a poisonous compound of terrorism, bigotry, greed and homeless misery.

Irony! Up the road from us a tall, handsome cherry tree is in glorious flower, 'wearing white', as the poet had it, 'for Eastertide'. Its bunched blossoms remind me of clusters of radars, rangefinders and such on the mainmast of a warship, so I have nicknamed it The Japanese Battleship.

DAY 104

I suppose it's crossed most of our minds, now and then, that perhaps Democracy is not such a good idea after all, especially now that the system seems unable to cope with the myriad miseries and political confusions of our times. I can well understand why Russians who grew up under the disciplines of Stalinist communism, Germans in the days of Hitler's National Socialism or even fascists in Italy felt somehow deprived when those arrogant systems fell, and their subjects were left groping for certainties with the rest of us. God knows, millions of them had suffered appallingly in the thrall of those regimes, but many more had undoubtedly felt secure and proud within the discipline of their despotisms. 'Ah,' I remember an Italian of my own age replying in 1946, when I remarked upon the vigorous splendours of Milan, 'ah, but you should have known it when Mussolini was here!'

If I do occasionally feel that a benevolent, cultivated, clever, artistic sort of dictator – a Churchill, for instance – might be a more welcome head of State than one of our run-of-the-mill prime ministers, I have only to remind myself of Winston's own dictum: that democracy is the worst form of human government except for all the others.

Nevertheless, not all the citizens who were loyal to those despotisms did so under ideological pressures. Many more of them, I feel sure, were not Nazis, or fascists, or communists. They were simply patriots.

I understand them, too. Believe me, I do not subscribe to that despicable credo 'my country right or wrong', but like most Britons of my age I generally assumed, in my youth, that Great Britain was usually right. Except for dauntless conscientious objectors, public opinion firmly supported Churchill when he promised the people, in the patriotic cause, only blood, toil and tears, and in that cause they generally accepted, if not autocracy, at least severe restrictions on their liberties. It was not a political ideology that sustained them, it was patriotism, and although that primitive, illogical emotion is half discredited today in Britain, nevertheless, right or wrong, in inspiration or in irony, it still has power.

When I came downstairs this morning I happened to notice a row of five elderly books on the bottom row of a bookcase. They were all entitled simply *The Royal Navy*, and it occurred to me that when they were published there was no need to say whose navy that was. It was the Navy, it was our navy, it was the British Navy, and like nearly everyone else I was proud of it.

Later in the day, I saw on the news an aerial picture of a squadron of the US Navy on its way to some miscreant destination – a carrier and half a dozen destroyers, ensigns fluttering, bow spray flying, in perfect formation in that distant sea.

I don't know what its mission was, just or squalid, but atavist that I am, I envied its ownership anyway.

DAY 105

Thinking still about democracy and such, I have been wondering why it is that the English, at least in our times, seem to have no hankering for a charismatic leader. Showy right-wing aspirants have fizzled out (think of Mosley), leftist heroes have not lasted long, Churchill himself they booted out of office once he had won the war. Heroes are not required, it appears, saints are not welcomed, and I cannot imagine a Trump winning an election here. Black and white is evidently too abrupt for the English public; pastels preferred.

So it is, it seems, that this exceptionally experienced democratic electorate prefers, as its national ikon, a totally irrational figure: a nobody in particular, untested and unexamined, from a not very gifted family, picked more or less at historical random out of a not especially successful pedigree. Sometimes the system works remarkably well; sometimes it is a dead loss. Either way, it apparently gives the English public satisfaction. It does not depend upon competition, rivalry or even aspiration. It is based upon the lottery of inheritance, and so far its philosophy, if one can call it that, has outstayed the ideologues.

I am an old republican, and I stand for a right little, tight little Wales without the absurdity of a hereditary monarch. But if the choice for England might be a Putin, a Kim Jong-un or even a Trump, let that old nation be singular, let it be quixotic, let it be entertaining, let it be fallibly human and stick to its well-tried nonsense.

Believe it or not, agnostic that I am, on Sunday I was quoted in a Calvinist Methodist service in the Capel y Traeth in Porthmadog, and these are the words attributed to me:

To my mind the fundamental engine of the Christian faith, as it is of most of the world's great religions, is the quality of kindness. It requires no exact definition. It is an essential aspect of all the great humanist qualities – mercy, forgiveness, generosity, unselfishness, even, at a pinch, humour. We need no theologian to expound it for us, no particular shining saint to exemplify it, because since childhood we have all experienced just what kindness is.

Fortunately, too, it is one of the few spiritual abstractions that is its own immediate reward. Being kind is not only, one might say, a stepping stone towards eternal recompense. It is itself an instant pleasure! It is fun! The kinder you are, the happier. Kindness is the very antithesis of those religious devices that, down the centuries, have required cruel sacrifices to achieve spiritual ends, like self-flagellations or fastings.

On the contrary, the more extravagant your kindnesses, the more joyous will be your welcome in heaven – and, oh dear, I rather fear the more swollen may be your own self-satisfaction! But never mind, your God's mercy is not strained. He will surely forgive a bit of swank in a just cause. So go on, be proud, be happy, be merciful, be grateful, be generous, be KIND.

I went to bed happy that night, bless their Calvinist hearts. Who knows? They may well be right.

DAY 107

When a reader writes to me about some writing of mine, I habitually answer the letter and slip it inside the volume concerned as a kind of memento (though too candid friends suggest I preserve only the flattering ones). Last week, I came across one which had been written some years before, and it greatly touched me in retrospect. I thought it would be nice to get in touch with its unsuspecting author, to thank him again for the letter and tell him that all these years later his response to my work was still giving me pleasure.

His telephone number was there at the top of his letter, and I rang it. There was no reply, but it was evidently still active, so instead I left a recorded message, thanking him for his kindness long before, wishing him well and hoping he was still enjoying the reading of books – perhaps even, I winsomely added, another one or two of mine . . . I gave him my telephone number too, in case he was amused enough to call me back.

He evidently wasn't – he never rang. However, now that I reread his original letter I see the reason why. 'I am long retired,' he had written at the bottom of the page, 'and now well into my nineties . . .'

Ah, what a sadness is there! My message had winged its way only to an emptiness. But I hope that perhaps, too late for this world, he may be listening to it in another, with a spectral chuckle.

DAY 108

Our half of the known world – the democratic part, that is, what we used to call the Free World – has been in a kind of maelstrom. From the Black Sea to the Baltic, it seems to have been enveloped in one vast and furious election. Polls have set upon us, generically as it were. The papers have been hijacked. TV illustrates nothing else. Every conversation is about one election or another, and a thousand politicians nag us to fulfil the duty of all conscientious citizens – to get out there and vote.

Before long, this immense drama will reach a climax in a British general election which will, as I understand it, permanently shift the so-called United Kingdom's status among the nations.

In the meantime, my allotted part has been to express an opinion in the election for membership of the district council of Dwyfor, within the county of Gwynedd, in Wales, and the Welshest corner of our country. I take fate seriously, and aware of my solemn responsibility at this evidently seminal moment in history, yesterday I drove down to the village hall to cast my vote. I felt that out of the immense cloud of suggestion that darkened the sky that evening, just for that exact moment history was summoning me. The Digit of Destiny was touching my very self – the Finger of Fate – as in top gear I arrived to play my allotted role in the great performance.

The village hall was closed. There was not an electoral placard in sight. Not a loudspeaker blared, nobody wore a rosette. When I asked why, they told me that since nobody wanted to oppose the candidate standing for Plaid Cymru, the Party of Wales, they did not see any point in having an election at all. The pub was open, though.

DAY 109

I don't know about you, but I like to have music in my car while I drive, and in our part of the world there are only two radio stations that fulfil my musical requirements. I don't want slush and I don't want rock or rap and I don't want anything tiresomely hackneyed or too experimental. I prefer something wonderful and slightly familar. Know what I mean? So I have become adept at switching between Classic FM and BBC Radio 3, and as I drive play the two of them contrapuntally. Here on 3, for instance, as my overture there is something rather lovely by a Lithuanian composer who's new to me, haunting, semi-Slavic stuff which takes me thoughtfully up Radio 3 to the end of the lane. Dear God, though, the next item on the programme is going to be a selection of medieval madrigals, the sort of music that has made my heart sink ever since I was weaned on Palestrina in my childhood. Quick – quick – over to Classic FM!

There they are playing something just a bit too hackneyed even for me – Rachmaninov or Mendelssohn, I would guess . . . But never fear, give it a moment and I'll bet you it will turn into something more freshly familiar. Wait! – there, you see? Hardly a minute's stop at the traffic lights and I am singing along with the radio a merry old Mozart melody . . .

Had enough? Want something definitive, so to speak, as we approach Tesco's and fumble for the debit card? Well, there's always the news on Radio 4.

DAY 110

The motions of transport concern me today, together with its aesthetic. Motion in itself is rather lovely – don't you think? – and most animals undertake it beautifully (not all – think of the crab or the poor pig). We human beings probably moved gracefully when we emerged from the Garden of Eden, and we still can, of course, when we try, but it is artificial modes of transport that concern me now. Humans riding horses often looked splendid, and navigating sailing ships was fine, but for my tastes the arrival of the machine muddied the immemorial beauties of human travel.

Steam did it first. I have never been an admirer of the steam age, which seems to me in retrospect a messy amalgam of soot, rust, smoke, iron, noise and clutter, however heroic the locomotives still seem to their devoted buffs.

But then came the airship and the aeroplane, and I have no grumble about them. Whether it has been by Concorde, Dreamliner or doomed Zeppelin, except for the clattering helicopter mankind's modern passage through the skies has been conducted with an elegance worthy of the ages.

And the automobile? Ah well, the car began in comical aesthetic ineptitude – did it not? – a clumsy stage coach without a horse, but today's cars seem to me, on the whole, remarkably graceful, if rather too noisy and, if there is such a word, emissive. Some of the greater machines of transport – the buses and the terrific showy trucks – seem as exciting to me as any old *Flying Scotsman*.

But wait, anyway! Do you hear that soft faint hum, gentle as the rub of silk on velvet, true as the whisper of heaven itself? That's the sound of transport's future, when – very soon, too! – the electric car takes over, making all else seem crude, selfish and coarse, and returning the practice of terrestrial travel to the serenity of the gods.

PS And if you believe all that, you'll believe anything.

DAY 111

For seventy-odd years I have lived, in love and in life, with my beloved friend Elizabeth, and only now is that subtle demon of our time, Dementia, coming between us.

She does not read these thoughts of mine, does not now read much really except catalogues and gardening magazines, and the scope of our conversation becomes narrower month by month. She forgets a lot, and crossly denies that she has forgotten it. She can still summon her old charm for outsiders, but saves her irritations for me.

And here's the subtlety of that damned demon. I know very well that her forgetfulness, her irritation, her narrowing interests are in no way her fault. I know it perfectly well, and I understand, but Dementia brings out the worst in me too. It is a two-way evil, and it incites me to harshness and impatience, and to say unpleasant things I really do not mean.

But here's a saving grace: I do not mean those calumnies, and Elizabeth knows it. Kindness reconciles us still, even when she is at her most irritating and I am at my nastiest, and in all our long years together, in life as in love, we have not once said goodnight without the sweet kiss of reconciliation.

Back to hell with you, Dementia!

DAY II2

Something tremendously awful happened to the world the other day. I cannot pretend to understand it, but it seemed that some extortionist malpractitioners, somewhere in the globe, by arcane cyber-techniques of ransom interfered directly with the private and public affairs of people and institutions in 150 countries.

All at once! In one day! One hundred and fifty countries! Millions of people speaking countless languages in every continent! Across all ideologies! Embracing all religions! Surely this is one of the seminal events of history? It evidently even caught up with me, when my debit card mysteriously declined to pay my bill at the Plough in Llanystumdwy last night. What is the world coming to?

Nobody seems to worry much around here. The chief complaint in the newspapers seems to be about the effect of this cataclysmic crime on the English National Health Service, never mind the effects on thousands of hospitals in China, Russia and, for all I know, inner Kazakhstan. There is much more in the news about football, local politics and President Trump.

Perhaps by the time you read this it will all be old news, more or less forgotten, but it lurks in my mind as a dreadful portent. If a handful of criminals can interfere with the peaceable lives and economies of 150 nations, think of the havoc still more wicked cyber-villains could wreak upon everyone's defences. Even their health. Even their moralities.

It doesn't bear thinking about.

DAY 113

Today, more about irony, that old preoccupation of mine.

I have always admired Winston Churchill's description of the British Grand Fleet sailing north to Scapa Flow at the start of the First World War. He said they were like 'giants bowed in anxious thought', and the phrase came pungently into my mind as I walked home up our lane yesterday. It was a classic Welsh evening of early summer: massed greens and speckled yellows, the lane dusty, the trees buoyant, the mountains dark blue and, yes, battleship grey on our horizon.

I am no giant, but I felt myself at one with those warships, for I was distinctly bowed in anxious thought. It happens, doesn't it? Quite suddenly, like an ultimatum, you find yourself clouded all around by worries, sadnesses and regrets.

In my case, on my evening walk, on the way home, my old friend irony stepped in. For how could it be, I thought, that into the idyll Nature had arranged for me, my little evening paradise, should intrude all those spectres of unhappiness? For those great old warships there was no irony. They were on their way to war, and some of them were presently to be sunk at Jutland. For me, well, 'Pull yourself together, Jan,' I said to myself, 'it's not the end of the world (I hope not anyway), you're not on your way to war (at ninety? Come on!), and by the nature of things irony is full of contradiction.'

When I got home I sought out a poem I vaguely remembered by Thomas Hardy. It begins very gloomily, concerning the poet's lugubrious thoughts about the miserable state of everything, but towards the end of the piece he is cheered up by the ecstatic sunset song of an 'aged thrush, frail, gaunt and small'.

It was just one word in the poem that I sought out this evening. Hardy tells us that the poor old bird, so gaunt and frail, 'flung' his soul against the prevailing gloom.

That's my thrush! There's another aspect of irony – its magical instructions! 'Stop moping about, Jan,' said I, as I put the book back, 'and get flinging!'

DAY 114

Today, 11 June 2017, I have to admit that, of all the days I have commemorated in this indolent sort of record, today the world around me seems to have reached some ultimate nadir. Wherever I look, east or west, up or down, inwards or outwards, searching the consolations of religion or the stimulants of art, in America as in Europe, in the war zones of Araby or the miserable refugee camps of Eritrea, everywhere I discern nothing but Chaos, with a capital 'C'. I cannot think it is the Ultimate Biblical Chaos – this is only my 114th thought, after all – and as a matter of fact, just at this moment, as I meditate over my cornflakes, there comes into my mind once more, as a kind of wry consolation, that old acronym of my wartime youth, long, long, long ago:

SNAFU.

Which meant Situation Normal: All Fucked Up.

Even then.

I am proud to be an honorary Fellow of the Royal Institute of British Architects, which gives me carte blanche, I tell myself, to sneer publicly at architects.

Not that I have often done it. Only once, in fact, when I turned up my nose at Richard Rogers's universally admired National Assembly building in Cardiff, on the grounds that it was insufficiently Welsh. But now I have come to feel that around the world too many architects no longer consider the city, surely their ultimate professional concern, to be itself a work of art, an emblem and declaration.

Earth had nothing to show more fair, thought Wordsworth, contemplating London from Westminster Bridge in 1802, but what would he think today, surveying the vulgar hodge-podge that would now meet his eye – the Shard and the Gherkin, the Heron Tower and the Cheesegrater and the Walkie-Talkie and a host of showily anomalous residential tower blocks, built with no apparent reference to one another, still less to the civic whole?

I suppose the first archetypically modernist conurbation was Manhattan, as it burgeoned with the advent of the skyscraper. Sensible planning restrictions governed its development, visionary architects contributed to its styles, and by the 1940s it truly was a thing of beauty, in distant silhouette as in street scene. It remains so today, no longer supreme in size or reputation, battered about a bit by history, but still a noble expression of human creativity.

Alas, it is no longer a universal criterion. Look at the new cities that have sprung up in our time. Take Doha, for example, one of the richest cities on earth, which I remember myself as an insignificant Arabian fishing village, and which is now, thanks to the profits of oil, a visual epitome of capitalist opportunism. It is a sea city, but seen from the sea it offers us no proud exemplar of mankind's noble enterprise, not even a monument to oil and its power, but just a preposterous parade of assorted shapes and substances, not unlike a child's tin of biscuits. The emergence of Doha as a city not just of wealth, but of countless cultural initiatives has found no architectural expression, no inspiring skyline, no noble Islamic allegory, no view from Westminster Bridge.

I know, I know, money is to blame, but money itself can have its dignity. Years ago I sailed into London on a ship from New York, and as we passed under Tower Bridge we saw the then modest but rather gloomily impressive buildings of the City, in those days still the financial capital of the world. '*That's* the City of London?' expostulated an American woman standing by me at the rail. 'My God, I expected more than that!' But to my mind architecture need not be pleasing to express its meaning – those buildings were grey and loveless, but so was the City of London, and the one expressed the other, as art and symbolism can.

Anyway, that's what I think. I think too many architects are concerned above all with profit and celebrity, rather than with art, or beauty, or aspiration, or philosophy, the human heart or the view from the bridge.

(Lord Rogers, by the way, gently wrote to remind me that his great-grandfather had been responsible for many of the best nineteenth-century constructions of Trieste, in particular the funicular railway to Opicina, which I am particularly fond of. Ever since his letter I have assiduously championed that Cardiff building of his, a fine, fine conception.)

DAY 116

I have been ill, hospitalized, bed-bound at home, enduring the queer delusions that can accompany kidney failures and feeling thoroughly sorry for myself. The kindest administrations of family, neighbours and friends have carried me through, and today, at last, praise God, I am going to drive my car again!

How faithfully it has been standing out there in the yard waiting for the summons, my dear old Honda Civic Type R, 2006 vintage and still the elderly boy racer's dream, with the leaves of autumn on its bonnet and the summer sunshine crinkling them – an old friend only waiting for a turn of the ignition key at last . . .

O dear, what if . . .? But no, the battery's fine, the handbrake's off, the six gears eagerly await my orders. I fasten my belt, squirm in my seat a little, and with the appropriate snarl we are off, skidding out of the yard, through the rickety gates, through the farmyard, up the bumpy drive, and like Mr Toad before me I am away. Away! Out on the highway with the whole wide world before me!

As it nears the end of its career, to be replaced by cleaner, more environmentalist successors, I would like, here and now, with a poisonous black burst from my exhaust and a vulgar toot upon my horn, to express my gratitude to the internal combustion engine, which did some dreadful things in its time, and is leaving some dire legacies behind, but which has given me and countless million others, Toads and all, the freedom of the open road.

DAY 117

O, I can imagine still the efforts of Great-Aunt Agatha, bedridden in her extreme old age, to find among her possessions a suitable birthday present for me, aged eight or so. I hardly knew her, and remember her not at all, but all my life I have felt the poignancy of unwrapping her little birthday parcel, to find within it a penknife so rusted with age that I was never able to open it.

What trouble she had taken, rooting among her drawers to find something to please a small child! How carefully she had cleaned it and wrapped it, and with her shaky old handwriting addressed it for the post – never once, in her life or in mine, to cut an apple.

And I am recalling it all the more vividly today because tomorrow is the ninth birthday of our granddaughter Begw, and temporarily bedridden as I am, and extremely old, I have thought of nothing better to give to her than a silly little rhyme I've thought up and a comic hybrid postcard I've stuck together, half of Stonehenge, half of Cricieth . . .

Will she be amused? Perhaps, but disappointed too at getting nothing better. Will she be grateful? Bless her heart, I am sure she will, and she will understand, as I did as I struggled with Great-Aunt Agatha's penknife, that the old lady's done her best.

Happy Birthday, Begw darling, and forgive me!

DAY 118

Well, dear friends, if ever there was a day that I felt like opting out of everything, it is today, 29 June 2017. Every single piece of news that reaches me from the wide world, here in our remote corner of Wales, speaks of conflict, disaster, deceit, tragedy, sadness, pathos. From Brussels to Brazil, poor old America to pathetic London, Trump to Kim Jong-un, Qatar and Yemen and Uganda and Mosul and Hong Kong, almost everywhere seems as irredeemably unhappy as everywhere else. It is astonishing to me that people have the stamina to engage in lifelong political or economic rivalries, and my guess is that millions like me, everywhere on the planet, sometimes feel like giving up.

To cap it all, in my own case, I watched on television yesterday the elaborate traditional ceremony in which the Queen of Great Britain and her dominions across the seas announces at Westminster her elected government's policies for the next session of the Mother of Parliaments. The elaborate style of this occasion, the historical allusions, the trumpets and the tapestries and the uniforms, the massed guards, the crown itself on its tasselled cushion and the aged monarch gamely reciting the manifesto are a deliberate demonstration of a nation's ancient traditions.

Not so very long ago it would have been the moving enactment of a great historical presence, too, presenting as in allegory, like it or not, the culmination of an immense and unique national achievement. Yesterday all its ancient splendours seemed to me at best nonsensical, at worst downright pathetic.

I turned off the television in sad despair and as an utter antidote played instead a cracked record I have of a song from an Australian musical comedy from long ago. It is raw, simple, honest, almost out of another age and another world. 'Blimey,' the song goes, 'I tilts my lid to yer, sweet Doreen, I'll be your bloke if you want, Doreen, you're the best kid that I've ever seen, I tilts my lid to Doreen . . .' – set to a boisterous old Aussie tune that I would whistle to you now, if I could, to cheer you up as it did me.

But no, you would probably only laugh bitterly, as would the poor old Queen, I suppose, or Kim Jong-un, or quarrelling politicians, or grasping financiers, or bigots and cynics and terrorists across the world.

What's the use of whistling? Hardly anyone does it nowadays.

How I wish – I really do – that I could appreciate contemporary rap music, if that's what it's called. It is at this moment, via my radio, reaching me from the Glastonbury Festival, and I can't make head nor tail of it. Is there meaning to it? Is there melody? What about it inspires its vast audiences to such instant rapture? I don't for a moment denigrate its worth; I only wish I could understand and share in it.

It's obviously a generational matter, and millions like me, I have no doubt, last really enjoyed the mass music of the day with the Beatles. But at the same time we were all moved and inspired by the art and intellects of people like Dylan, Bowie and the enigmatic Leonard Cohen, interweaving, as it were, the paving stones of Abbey Road. Do they have their equivalents today? Am I missing some musical exegesis of the times, to tell me how the light gets in? Is it me? Am I the Philistine?

Perhaps that cacophony of Glastonbury is a truth in itself, its own loveless zeitgeist. Or, please God, will the times soon be a-changin'?

DAY 120

I don't know if I have mentioned before my envy of Ovid. Having read about his exile from Rome by the Emperor Augustus in AD 8, some years ago I resolved to make a detour to the Black Sea town of Tomis, in Romania, where he spent his last years and wrote much of his immortal poetry. It is called Constanţa nowadays, and I loved it. I thought then that, really, if one has to be exiled, what better than to spend one's last years writing poetry in a garden beside the sea?

Well, Ovid has entered my thoughts again now because I have entered a sort of temporary exile myself. Incapacitated by sickness, overwhelmed by worries material, familial and philosophical, I have declared myself *hors de combat* for the time being, declining commissions, fighting off visitors and going nowhere. And I was right! It has been delightful! I now know our own garden, as Ovid doubtless knew his, better than I have ever known it, in detail as in the whole, from the sweetest violet to the grand old sycamore that dominates the scene; and the blackbirds that frequent it, the pigeons, the elegant naughty magpies and the squirrels seem more than ever like family friends.

All I do all day is record these occasional thoughts, in my own time, to my own length. I earn practically nothing, but then I don't spend much either. I am like the vestal virgins of old, the world forgetting, by the world forgot.

The emperor never did relax his sentence, but my own Ovidian experience will presently come to an end, like my illness and my incapacitation, and I shall no longer be vestal virginal. The telephone will ring again, the Internet will baffle me once more and all the world's corrosions will resume their whittlings. Goodbye, magpies, you dear scoundrels! Au revoir, Sir Sycamore!

* * *

Yes, yes, I'll call you back. Monday morning, did you say? How many words? Hang about – someone at the door. Great to hear from you – I'm sure we can work something out. You'll let me know? Keep in touch. Tuesday, did you say? Drop me an e-mail. What? Who? How d'you spell it?

DAY 121

A PS from yesterday, especially for anyone who has suffered the same kidney attacks as I lately have. A strange thing happened while I was recently in hospital. I was waiting for an available bed in a ward, and in the meantime loitered about in the crowded public spaces. During the evening, two elaborately antique horse-drawn coaches made their difficult way through the rooms towards the rear, obviously on their way to some sort of festival or exhibition.

Nobody could tell me what they were, or where the show was to be, and next day, when I was comfortably in bed in my ward, I asked my kind nurse what the occasion had been.

There was no occasion, she said. There had been no ornate horse-drawn coaches. It was all hallucination, a phenomenon not uncommon, I now know, among the multiple symptoms of kidney trouble. So don't be surprised, my dear fellow sufferers, if baby elephants infest your bathroom, or you get a letter from the Queen of Sheba. It will pass. They are but kidney-dreams.

Drop me a line about them, if you like, c/o my cousin Abraham Lincoln, Arsenal Football Club, Llanystumdwy, Wales.

DAY 122

Today the Prime Minister of Great Britain is off to Hamburg, to a meeting of her international peers, the so-called G20 group of the world's chief nations. How I pity her! Not so long ago it would have been her duty to represent before the world an ancient State of unparalleled experience, confidence and prestige, rich, powerful, influential – a country like no other, playing a part in history's drama that was unique and dramatic. Alas, poor Mrs May, as she takes her place today among her contemporaries. Gone is the charisma that would have attended her predecessors, and which indeed attended all her compatriots, me included, in the days when we thought of ourselves as pioneers and champions of democracy, and a victorious people too, a people with a mighty past, a great manufacturing people, an innovative people, the people of Churchill and Shakespeare, Oxford and Cambridge, world-celebrated scientists and sportsmen, a nation famous at once for its humour and for its poetry! How much of all that will attend poor Mrs May, as she takes her place among the virile modernist States of today, the Americans and the Germans and the Chinese and the Russians, whose finances rule the world now, and whose ambitions are boundless?

It is not that the United Kingdom (née Great Britain) has disgraced itself. It has simply, it seems to me, lost the gift of greatness. Almost deliberately, by its own actions, it has relegated itself to the minor ranks of the nations, and ensured, I suspect, that when Queen Elizabeth's prime minister addresses her peers in Hamburg this week, some of them will be a little sorry for her too.

Sorry for the British! Dear God! What *have* they come to?

DAY 123

Did you hear me crying yesterday? I really was reduced to tears by that unwitting instrument of harassment, my computer. During the morning a man called me out of the blue to tell me what I must urgently do if I wanted to keep it working. I didn't know there was anything wrong with it, but the man explained that there were technical faults in our area that needed urgent attention to prevent my computer service being switched off altogether. He was gently polite, and helpful, but spoke in so extreme a foreign accent that I could not make out just what he wanted of me – what I must do to keep online (e.g. press the CTRL button on my keyboard, while simultaneously pressing the buttons E and PGDN), or why I must please stay online while his technical colleagues put things right. He himself was always there to help, he said.

All day long – literally! – that man and various anonymous assistants pestered me, hour after hour, with telephone calls and numerical reminders and obscure technical warnings. They never let up, until in the end I was exhausted, reduced to tears and defeated. Limply and ridiculously, against all my better judgement, I told them details of my economic circumstances that I (I and you too, I expect) had been specifically warned never to reveal. I told them everything they wanted, almost as though I had been hypnotized. Perhaps in a sense I had?

During the night I realized what I had done, and this morning I rang everyone to cancel everything. With luck, please God, touch wood, no harm has been done. I had woken from my lachrymose trance in time to reproach myself for my foolishness, and to curse those villains, who- ever and wherever they are, for taking cruel advantage of a harmless old soul like me.

They rang again this morning, but now I answered them differently. May they rot in their own cyber-shit.

DAY 124

An elderly lady sitting in her wheelchair on the pavement this morning solicited my contribution to whatever worthy charity she represented. I had no notes in my purse, and I regretfully told her so, but when I had walked on a few yards I did find a few coins in the bottom of my bag. I went back to put them in her collecting box, and apologized for their meanness. I honestly had no more, I told her – honestly!

Did she forgive me? Did she say thank you, anyway? Did she even smile? She did not, the old grumps. But there she was, sitting there in the morning cold, serving a good cause, and I was on my way, as a matter of fact, to treat myself to an excellent cappuccino, for which I would pay with my credit card. So on the whole I think the balance of merit was hers, don't you?

At the entrance to our village of Llanystumdwy, on the north-west coast of Wales, a sign directs the traveller to Lloyd George Grave. I often wonder how many strangers, especially foreigners, know what it means. Lloyd George Grave? Who was he? What was he? He was a politician, and the reputations of politicians are not always as eternal as they may have hoped.

I fear David Lloyd George, one of the most famous of all Welshmen, may be an example. He is certainly not forgotten in Llanystumdwy, but to the motorists hastening by down there, how much does the name mean to them, as they hurry by our signposts? A thousand actors and actresses are better remembered – today's *Sun* newspaper, as it happens, actually leads its front page with the headline that a woman is to be the next Dr Who of the TV series, far outranking any news of war, politics, economics, command or statesmanship!

Nevertheless, dear reader, whether you be from Reykjavik, Miami or Leatherhead, if you pass by our village do take a moment to visit Lloyd George Grave. It is the peaceful resting place of a man who was once tremendous. In a kind of grotto the Welshman David Lloyd George lies, beneath a boulder beside our little River Dwyfor where he liked to sit and meditate. As you pause there yourself you may remember that he once dictated the fate of armies, of nations even, in the days long ago when a prime minister of imperial Britain commanded much of the world, and decreed the fate of millions.

Lloyd George grew up in a little cottage up the road, but he became one of the most famous men on earth. I don't suppose much of his dust is still floating around his grotto there, but you might perhaps recall, before you saunter back to your car, what another visitor murmured at another burial place: 'Imperious Caesar, dead, and turned to clay, might stop a hole to keep the wind away.'

PS In my library I have Lloyd George's signed copy of an *Atlas of the Historical Geography of the Holy Land* (London, 1915). As prime minister, in 1917 he gave another copy of it to General Sir Edmund Allenby, to encourage that officer when he set off with his British imperial army to capture Jerusalem from the infidel Turks. The wind blew there too.

DAY 126

The longer I live, the more I love my library, and this is lucky, because it is a terrible time-waster. I enjoy nothing more than just pottering about in it, picking out a volume now and then simply to renew its acquaintance, or in the hope of finding a letter from an old friend tucked in its pages, or to remind myself of a phrase I remember with particular pleasure or an observation that maddened me forty years ago – will it madden me still, or was it a callow judgement? I love just handling my books, sorting them a bit better by subject or by size, or apologizing to one when space or shape obliges me to stack it flat on its side in a bookshelf instead of standing tall – such a demeaning destiny, I always think. Waste of time, certainly, but now that I have, as it were, half withdrawn from the world, what an infinite pleasure to have such a host of old associates in the house – and new ones too, for one of the few perks of the writer's life is the endless supply of books that want to be reviewed! (There used to be bookshops in London that specialized in buying used review copies from impecunious young critics. I wonder if there still are – perhaps impecuniosity is not what it was?)

Not many of my books are very valuable, anyway, but they are great companions, and they are *mine*! Only a few have I inherited: some of the old classics, *Huck Finn* and the King James Version and a Dickens or two and a set of Balzac and the mildewed memoir about his Egyptian experiences that my great-great-grandfather privately published in 1877.

All the rest I have acquired for myself, and as I have always written in them where I got them and when, they have become an intimate kind of record of my life – a grand reminder, if you like. As a visitor to our house observed long years ago, they are like so many friends sitting there in their stacks, and they have matured or declined along with me – when I laugh they laugh, when I cry they shed a tear, they can be as maudlin as I sometimes am and just as cheerful too.

And if they are often out of date, well, bless their hearts, so am I.

DAY 127

In a miserably naughty world, here most decidedly is a doer of good deeds. A lifelong friend and neighbour of ours dropped in last night to tell us about her recent journey to Australia. She had undertaken it because her husband badly wanted to see his own expatriate brother once again, and the snag was this: that her beloved husband himself, recently rescued from death by drastic cancer surgery, has no stomach and can be fed only via injection.

Did this deter our doer of good deeds? Did it hell! From Wales the two of them took the train to London, from London they flew to Dubai, from Dubai to Perth. It is almost 9,000 miles as the crow flies, and they flew economy class – there and back! Can you imagine the misery of it? The airport queues, the immigration checks, the baggage inspections, the boarding of buses, the getting of taxis, the queuing at counters, the fumbling for passports – and every now and then, I can only suppose, that remorseless but life-preserving syringe.

They got home safely, anyway, and here was that dauntless old friend telling us about the journey as though they had just been down to Cardiff to see the rugby. God (if there is one), take note.

DAY 128

Birds puzzle me enough, heaven knows (and even mystify ornithologists, when it comes to migrations), but I am still more baffled by butterflies. What *are* they about? We have only a fairly ordinary selection of them fluttering about our place, and as it happens the kind that particularly intrigues me is the most ordinary, the common-or-garden white sort. I take this to be the Cabbage White listed in W. S. Coleman's *British Butterflies* (1896, downstairs in my library, next to *The Dodo and Kindred Birds*), if only because Cabbage White seems the right sort of name for the run-of-the-mill insects I am talking about. The more elegant specimens that sometimes visit our garden, which I take to be Red Admirals, or perhaps Painted Ladies, appear to comport themselves in a logical way as they move from plant to plant for sustenance; it is the Cabbage Whites that seem to me to be bonkers.

They generally come in pairs, and they cavort meaninglessly around the place, only occasionally pausing to visit a flower of some sort, just for a second or two, but mostly just aimlessly swooping here and there, or suddenly breaking away from each other at terrific speed for no apparent reason. Their power-to-weight ratio must be extraordinary – I reckon that sometimes, sporadically, they must be moving at forty miles an hour up there, before they apparently lose heart, or vigour, and subside into a listless flutter.

What *is* it all about? Can a species have no conscious purpose at all? Coleman takes it all in his encyclopedic stride, but when the other afternoon I asked a visiting Red Admiral what on earth the Cabbage Whites were all about, he simply did the butterfly equivalent of a tap on the side of the head.

Here, for once, is a pleasant surprise for an old fogey. I have lately become averse to most things televisionic, from news bulletins to drama serials, with the result that I am, as it were, half illiterate by contemporary standards. Like President Trump (for once), I suspect much of the news I get on the TV channels to be Fake, and many of the so-called experts to be overpaid phonies. As for S*tar Wars* and *The West Wing* and even *Downton Abbey*, with such as them I am altogether out of my depth, and if I had not been left cold by Bilbo and the hobbits when they were characters in a novel, I surely would have been by their reincarnations on the silver screen.

So it is hardly surprising that Harry Potter and co., J. K. Rowling's worldwide blockbusting creations, should not have entered my field of acquaintance until last night. Last night? Last night, and even then not between book covers. After supper, when I turned on at random my despised television, I found myself bowled over by a brilliant Anglo–US film adaptation of one or other of her novels. I don't know which one it was, but it seemed to have its full complements of wizards and school champions and villains and magic plots, and it seduced me.

Technically, it was obviously brilliant, as even I could see, with amazing camera angles, cuts and perspectives, but artistically too it seemed to me wonderful. This was partly because throughout the film eminent English actors and actresses appeared incongruously disguised, invariably bringing to the performance a taste of classy diction. It was partly because the entire cast of supporting actors and bit players seemed to me wonderfully convincing. But it was chiefly because the very conception of the whole fantasy, paper to screen, struck me as a work of high art.

It was a totally unexpected delight. I am late in recognizing the stature of the work, and I realize too that by now some of those young actors, strangers to me, are international stars themselves. But I'm not too late to pull myself together, recognize a brave new genre (well, fairly new) and even have another go at those hobbits.

Every morning I take my breakfast (muesli, tea, toast and bitter marmalade) out of the kitchen into the library, where I eat it – alone, Elizabeth being still in bed.

There is a ceremonial aspect to this procedure. The marmalade is a different one every morning of the week, from a rack of seven; the tea is Twining's English Breakfast; the muesli is Special Fruit and Nut; and my breakfast tray began life as a communication from the editors of *Rolling Stone* magazine in New York, who years ago sent me a hand-drawn alphabet of their elegant new typeface, signed by its designer with a courteous message. I had this converted into a tray with gilded handles, and upon it, every morning, I carry my victuals from one room to the other. So, as you see, the occasion is not without ceremony.

Yesterday, though, for no particular reason, it did occur to me what fun it would be to drop the whole caboodle on the floor, all of it – English Breakfast, Fruit and Nut, Ty Newydd Special Marmalade, *Rolling Stone* Old Style, gilt-handled tray and all. Instant crash chaos, with its ingredients spreading in a sticky slush from one room to the other! Wouldn't that be worth a Thought?

It was not altogether original. From long ago I remember a Hollywood farce in which one of the great comedians of the day – Danny Kaye? – pulled an immensely long tablecloth off a table laid with infinite splendour for some inconceivably grand dinner. He did it with a single explosive tug, sending not just the dinner-table crockery, but the whole preposterous occasion into shattered ridicule. I loved that outrageous performance, and ever since I have told myself, now and then, that when the time came, I would do it myself.

I did it yesterday, as a matter of fact, but it was only in my mind. I ate my breakfast decorously, as usual, so Elizabeth in her cosy bed had no idea of the marvellous slapstick that was being mentally enacted next door, and never actually got up to find a viscous mass of marmalade, tea and muesli oozing turgidly from one room to another.

Another time!

DAY 131

I am ashamed that I have not been to the Welsh National Eisteddfod this week – especially as, peripatetic as it is, it is taking place this year on the island of Anglesey, not far from us. What makes me the more ashamed is the fact I am proud to be a member of the *Gorsedd*, the governing body of the Eisteddfod. Worse still, in recent years I have let slip my grasp of the Welsh language, which is the whole *raison d'être* of the institution. My forgiving son Twm says I faltered in my use of *yr hen iaith* after I had brain surgery some years ago, and he may be right. But that's really no excuse, and I am sorry.

O my goodness, I forgot, perhaps you have never heard of the Eisteddfod. It is a week-long festival of music and the arts which is descended from immemorial traditions of the Welsh culture, and which in its present form has been celebrated annually since 1881. It happens in a different Welsh location every year, north and south alternately, and is said to be the biggest such celebration of a nation's culture in Europe. It certainly grips Welsh-speakers (some half a million of them) with passionate enthusiasm. Much of my own family is in Anglesey at this moment, on the rain-sodden field that is this year's site (and which will be remembered always by the mystic circle of stones that every national Eisteddfod leaves behind it).

227

The occasion dominates the Welsh-language media, so at least I have been able to participate, sort of, via television. As always, it has moved me greatly. Of course, there is much to deplore in our country, even the Welshest aspects of it, but not just now, not this week. So many eager, honest faces are there on the screen, singing their hearts out or declaiming poetry in the stylized theatrical manner that is endemic to the occasion: fresh young children's faces, earnest and determined, or the middle-aged, enthusiastic faces of ladies' choirs, or the stern, resolute faces of the massed bravos, old and young, whose male-voice choirs have made their art a very epitome of Welshness down the generations.

They must be a mixed lot really, I know that – the children a nuisance sometimes, the ladies catty, the gentlemen of the choirs not always gentlemanly at all – but to me this week, as I sit shamefaced before my TV screen, they all seem to be people to be proud of, people to love and to be grateful for, like the little nation they represent and its ancient lyrical language.

It's the last day of the Eisteddfod today, and Suki and Meilyr are dropping in for tea at Trefan, on their way home to Goginan.

Today is the first Monday in August 2017, and it must be for ever remembered as a *dies horribilis* in the annals of Charlottesville, Virginia, one of the most delightful small cities in America. I have been interested in the place for half a lifetime, because I loved it when I first turned up there in the 1950s, because I have dear friends there, and because it has always seemed to me a kind of paradigm of decent Americanness.

It was the home, for a start, of President Thomas Jefferson, chief author of the Declaration of Independence and a man of civilized resource. He founded the University of Virginia there and himself designed for it what are, for my money, the most delightful academic buildings in America, besides creating one of the most delightful houses, his home of Monticello up the road.

Then again, I liked Charlottesville at once because it seemed to me to speak of the style, the romance and the dash of the old American South. Looking back now, seventy years on, I am more aware that the style, dash, etc., had essentially been the dash and style of the slave-owning Confederate South. But so what? I put that out of my mind, I suppose, and when I came across a jolly song about Robert E. Lee, the final Confederate commander, the slavists' champion, I assumed it referred to a Mississippi steamboat of that name, which had won a famous river race in 1870. I was often disconcerted by prejudices in the USA of the 1950s, but as I remember it, not particularly in Charlottesville . . .

Alas, after today the place will always be remembered differently, even by me, because today's savage rioting in the city did arise out of that old American curse – race. Would you believe it, today's calamity really began with the Civil War of a hundred and fifty years ago, and specifically with Robert E. Lee, my steamboat man? The city fathers had recently decided that his statue, in one of the main squares of the city, should be removed – he was, after all, a hero specifically of the slave-owning South and, indeed, an owner of black slaves himself. This decision has infuriated right-wing white racists, Ku Klux Klanists, neo-Nazis and such; and so, what with one development and another, the revival of age-old prejudices and resentments burst into hideous violence, and thus added today's ugly page to the annals of sweet Charlottesville.

What a mess! Where do I stand? The city fathers were honouring, I suppose, their own liberal principles – good on them, and I am told that all over the South such statuary often does deliberately honour the ugly principle of white supremacy. But if to be a slave-owner in the nineteenth century was to be a sinner in the American memory, then Tom Jefferson, to my simple mind the very soul of Charlottesville itself, was a false idol. Who said history was bunk?

DAY 133

Now here's an innocent cameo, in a world where innocence, just at the moment, seems in short supply.

I stand beside our garden gate, waiting for the postman to come on his morning rounds when he has collected the outward mail from the postbox at the end of the lane. I have done something foolish, being slightly senile these days: last night I posted in that box four postcards, in reply to four strangers who had written to me about my work, and in my fuddled way I had mixed them all up and addressed each card to the wrong recipient.

'Never get old!' say I to the postman, when he rolls up in his red van, but he is quick to comfort me. He has with him last night's outward mail, says he, to take to the sorting office, and yes, he says, fumbling in his big canvas bag, here are my postcards, virgin mail, so to speak, unspoilt and unsullied, and he gives them back to me to readdress, and we laugh, and he kids me, and all is well. How lucky I am, think I, to live and work among friends.

But it seems to me, nevertheless, that he is not quite his benign self. Is he, at heart, just a little irritated by my inefficiency? Could it be, I wonder, that he was disobeying some Post Office regulation in giving me back my mail? But no. It was his dog, he confesses to me, that is on his mind – his dear old dog, a friend for many years, whom he has just taken to the vet, perhaps for the very last time.

He will get a diagnosis, he tells me, wiping away the suggestion of a tear and declining a quick whisky, when he finishes his rounds this morning – and his hand waves bravely from the window of his van as he drives away through the dusty potholes.

O the world may be out of joint, and sadness reigns, but decency still lurks there all the same, up by all our garden gates.

The other day I broadcast a programme on the BBC, and I'll tell you why I did it: I was sorry for the United States of America!

Everyone I knew there – lifelong friends, recent acquaintances, strangers who wrote to me for one reason or another – every American seemed to be downcast, despondent and dismayed, like the distorted lyrics of an old song, by the condition of their country.

We all know that the USA has never been perfect. Indeed, in our own time it has sometimes been downright horrid, in public life as in private goings-on. It has plastered the world with influences that were often degrading, and has sometimes led us all into catastrophe. But I have loved the old republic for most of a lifetime, and it has saddened me to see it not only behaving badly and unsuccessfully, but *knowing* it. I admired its old swank and panache, and I wanted to do something to revivify the idea of America and remind us all of its happier times – the 1960s, say, when it was still flushed, beloved, generous and victorious in the aftermath of the Second World War.

Part of my broadcast was a slightly soppy and sentimental reminiscence of my own relationship with the USA at that time, but partly it was a sort of musical potpourri of 1960-ish Americanisms. Here are the seven compositions I chose for uplift: 'Shenandoah', 'Chattanooga Choo

Choo', 'The Folks Who Live on the Hill', 'New York, New York', 'Come Home', 'One for My Baby', 'Give Me Your Tired, Your Poor'.

And here are the artists represented: Liza Minnelli, Glenn Miller, Frank Sinatra, Rodgers and Hammerstein, Jerome Kern, Peggy Lee, Irving Berlin, Cincinnati Pops Orchestra, the Mormon Tabernacle Choir, Felix Mendelssohn.

'Felix Mendelssohn?' I hear you expostulate. 'Felix *Mendelssohn*?' Why not? Was not that grand old America welcoming to one and all? Wasn't that the point of it?

This morning I drove my Elizabeth into town to have her hair done, and on the way she warned me, as she often does, that I should keep more to the right, or more to the left, I forget which. I was about to remind her testily how long I have been driving a car when this memory came into my mind:

Years ago, in London, I was driven back to my hotel, after lunch, by a very well-known novelist, now long dead. She was of a certain age, a little shaky, and as we approached the traffic maelstrom of Hyde Park Corner I ventured to ask her if she was OK to drive through it. 'My dear Jan,' she haughtily replied, 'I have been driving around Hyde Park Corner for seventy years, and I should know my way around it by now . . .'

So, no, I did not reply haughtily to Elizabeth this morning. I did what she suggested, whatever it was, and remembered instead what old John Donne taught us all: 'for whom the bell tolls; it tolls for thee'.

DAY 136

One of the fascinations of Wales is the fact that it has two languages, a circumstance not always cherished even by many of its own inhabitants, but to my mind lovely. Yesterday a friend coming to tea with us brought along her bilingual five-year-old son, who, between hearty mouthfuls of cake, prattled convivially on about his affairs and preoccupations of the moment.

He is a delightful little fair-haired boy, and he brought with him, I thought, a particular kind of elegance. Fluent as he is, sometimes he chose to use a Welsh word, sometimes an English one, and there were momentary pauses in his discourse while he considered which. Perhaps he was not sure that he had got the word itself right, in one language or the other, but I preferred to think that his pause was a matter of art or instinct, and I thought there was something truly beautiful in those moments of silent hesitation, poised between two ancient tongues – as though, thought I, he was in touch with angels.

What a load of nonsense, I tell myself now, but I am tempted all the same to quote Gregory the Great's famous dictum, '*Non Angli, sed Angeli*,' except that '*Angli*' most certainly will not do . . .

I'm not entirely sure yet, but I think I must opt out of the world's affairs. Yesterday I was invited to write an article for a well-known London publication, and I replied thus: 'It's very kind of you to think of me, but to be honest I can't be bothered.' I expected a stiff reply, but when it came, by instant e-mail, it was simply, 'Bravo!'

On the other hand, I have been reading this morning, as I always do with my cornflakes, the *Guardian*'s correspondence columns. Today several scores of readers contributed their opinions on world affairs. Some wrote learnedly, some crudely, some rudely, some passionately, some preposterously and a few evidently so outrageously that the editors found it necessary to expunge their contributions. I must assume that all of them, though, wrote at all because they thought their opinions could somehow affect the state of the world – as indeed at a pinch they might, I suppose, when filtered through the infinite mesh of democratic politics.

I am not of their company, though. I used to write letters quite frequently to *The Times*, but few of them were published, and as I remember it they were mostly to express outrage at monarchical flamboyances. Today I don't care how royalty displays itself, and for that matter can hardly summon the phlegm to spit at anyone else, so you will not find my name on any newspaper's letter page (unless, of course, it be in the *Caernarfon and Denbigh Herald*).

As for the multifarious controversies that so excite the readers of the *Guardian* today, well, I confess they are beyond my ageing ken. I have only recently learnt that Myanmar is what Burma used to be. I am really past caring if Mrs May is going to win the next election, or if President Macron has been spending too much on make-up, or if President Trump is going to be impeached, or if a man called Kim, who I always thought was a beloved character of fiction, is likely to attack the island of Guam with a nuclear-armed rocket, or if the National Health Service will go bust because of its expenditure on demented old folk, or if the Royal Navy is investing in immense outmoded warships, or if world-respected athletes turn out to be corrupt, or if the Chinese are taking over Asia, or if the Russians go in for cyber-spying, or any other of the numberless issues that excite the press, Twitter, Facebook, etc., and all those fervent subscribers to what I still prefer to think of as the *Manchester Guardian*, RIP.

I am mentally, spiritually, artistically, intellectually and possibly historically disqualified from useful participation in these debates and confrontations, and so I have half reached the conclusion that I should opt out. Am I on my own, or do I hear muted applause, like the tears of that baby behind the screen in the 1920 cartoon, crying for the future?

DAY 138

I blush to admit it, as a republican of long, long standing, but it seems to me that the one possible instrument of world peace is the quaint, ridiculous but essentially harmless British monarchy. The United Nations seems to have bowed out of the reconciliation business, all the Powers are absurdly quarrelsome, and the only diplomatic approach that every head of State seems eager to accept is an invitation from the Queen of England.

The difficulty is this: who is to offer such hospitality without being, or seeming to be, politically animated? I suggest somebody altogether detached from power, politics or economic dispute, somebody essentially innocent and even a bit simple, somebody of a certain age who has grown out of ambition or religious bias and only wishes to be *nice* – an unfashionable quality, but one I respect.

In short, somebody like me, and when invited I shall go at once to North Korea, for a start, to be nice to President Kim, to jolly him along and to take with me a sweetly worded invitation to spend a weekend at Balmoral with Her Majesty the Queen of England.

Who can doubt that he would accept, and it would be the gentle start of a universal diplomatic rapprochement, gratefully to be remembered by future generations as *Pax Janica*.

DAY 139

Yesterday was the opening day of Festival No. 6. It is a celebration of arts, music and such – you know what festivals are – which happens every year in the fanciful village of Portmeirion, a few miles from us down the north-west coast of Wales. The event takes its name, footlingly, I always think, from a sequence in a television programme called *The Prisoner*, which was filmed there years ago. I never watched it, and I am not big on festivals, but annually since this one began I have contributed to it a talk about Portmeirion itself.

This is because for seventy years and more I have frequented and enjoyed the highly idiosyncratic village itself, and for half a century at least I delighted in the company of its equally idiosyncratic inventor, Sir Bertram Clough Williams-Ellis, who died in 1978. Clough, as he was known to one and all, created the place from scratch, a light-hearted assembly of buildings old, reconstructed and brand new, assembled in a marvellous coastal site below the mountains of Snowdonia. It had a serious purpose – to demonstrate that it was perfectly possible to create a new tourist destination in a heavenly setting without wrecking the local numen – and it has worked perfectly ever since (except perhaps for visitors without a sense of humour . . .).

It has worked especially well for me – I take visitors there, I eat meals there, I love strolling about the place and enjoying its infinite subtleties of architecture and allusion. So when I learnt years ago that Festival No. 6 was going to be launched there, my heart sank. You know what festivals are! Portmeirion was sure to be spoiled, I thought, its delicate purposes ignored in the name of Profit, in an unsuitable site that was, for all its beauties, almost ignobly subject to our legendary Welsh weather, especially in early autumn. Poor Clough! thought I. Poor muddy Portmeirion!

And if you came to Portmeirion yesterday, you might have thought I was right. As usual, rain intermittently poured and mud was everywhere. A maelstrom of traffic infested the place amidst the puddles, with stern car-park warnings and myriad attendants and shuttle buses perpetually changing gear, and the whole village itself apparently taken over by some tented army of irregulars. When I picked my way towards the gloomy-looking marquee where I was to perform my piece, it was as though I was navigating Dante. Everywhere along my path, it seemed to me, were twisted backpack denizens of inferno, lying around in every corner of shelter, drinking from paper cups, weirdly dressed, and sometimes accompanied by violent, subhuman music.

But –

But! One and all, without exception, all those figures from hell, there amidst the mud and rain, turned out to be delightfully friendly and helpful. Holding their horrible coffee in one hand while they jumped to their feet to help me through some particularly ugly quagmire, they were laughing and smiling always, and truly kind; and so was my audience, when I arrived at last, dripping, confused and breathless, at my makeshift podium.

I could not have asked for a more understanding or forgiving reception to my address, when I floundered through it in that Dantean tent; and when I left Portmeirion in the evening, leaving the place to its own multifarious performances, I felt sure that far into the night dear old Clough himself would once again be enjoying the infernal goings-on. I always feel that in the end.

I have been, in my time, an old-school British imperial patriot, a groping liberal internationalist and a whole-hog Welsh nationalist, and I feel myself to be a bit of all of them to this day. Since I came of age at the end of the Second World War and Churchill was, so to speak, pensioned off, no politician has ever inspired me to say, 'Yes, that's it, that's a track to follow through the wilderness of our times.'

Until this morning, when I read that Jean-Claude Juncker of Luxembourg, the president of the European Commission, stood for a Federal Europe – an association far more ethereal than the loveless European Union. I have articulated the same ideal when people have asked me just what my own vague ideology envisaged. I have long said I stood for an independent Wales within a Federal Britain within a Federal Europe within (I have added, just to show I'm merely dreaming) a Federal World. But, yes, surely a Federal Europe is a perfect possibility, and perhaps the best we can aim at.

It is obvious to everyone, I assume, that the balance of world power is shifting, that traditional democracy is in decline, and that perhaps more than any other nation Britain is feeling the rot. No other country was so wedded, economically as well as intellectually or emotionally, to the idea of imperial greatness, and no other people, so far as I can see, has been so thoroughly thrown off balance by its own decline.

Surely, then, to be once more members of a great supranational power, a federation of equals, friends and colleagues, each still with its own national quirks, methods and characteristics, but each subscribing to a common ideology, with at least overlapping histories in common, and by now, as never before, a familiarity with each other's ways and habits – surely this is a noble aspiration.

So lead on, Herr Juncker (if 'Herr' you be, as a Luxembourger). If nobody else signs on, there is always me, a simplistic romantic, here in Llanystumdwy, Cymru/Wales, British Federation, Europe, the World.

DAY 141

I am at once pleased and regretful to record that our mouse infestation has been defeated. It was centred upon the corner of our kitchen where breads and cereals are stored, and so amounted, as it were, to an assault upon our very survival, together with a sort of chemical offensive upon our health mounted by very small black droppings of shit. Well, the attack has been repelled. First Elizabeth caught a mouse in a mousetrap, and threw it dead upon a rubbish tip; then I surprised one that was very much alive, head down in a packet of cornflakes, and banished it to the farthest corner of the garden.

Pleased, then, I certainly am, but sort of sorry too, because it turns out that those two little animals constituted the whole mass of our invasion. Since we disposed of them a month ago the mueslis and breads have been inviolate – not a single nibble or excrement among the loaves. It turns out that it was just the two of them, just two small, sorry creatures with as much right to life and self-sustenance as we have ourselves.

Thank God we've got rid of them, and if the live one finds its way back, I'll murder it.

DAY 142

Walking home yesterday on a lovely autumn evening I heard a deep rumble somewhere, and lumbering into my line of sight across an empty blue sky came an old-school helicopter – not one of your fancy hoppity sort that carry rich folk to their pleasures or their offshore profits, but the real thing, the original, the rumbling, labouring kind of helicopter that seems to me one of the great institutions of our time.

For good or for bad, that old thing up there (for it always strikes me as elderly) has been an inescapable contemporary ikon. It has outlived Concorde and the hovercraft, it has fought in wars and made innumerable rescues, it has provided employment for princes and escapes for dictators – hope and despair and pleasure and even comedy, all have been provided by that essentially ungainly mechanism.

Ungainly but to my mind heroic, in a homely kind. I know nothing about helicopters really, but they seem to me bee-like – bumblebee-like – and when that mechanism rumbled across my sky yesterday, going who-knows-where on who-knows-what category of mission, I would have tipped my hat to it in neighbourly friendship, had I been quite sure it was not going to machine-gun me.

DAY 143

Oxford, declared an American long ago, is a place where too many bells are ringing in the rain. It might almost be said, too, that it is a place where too many organs are always playing somewhere, in so many college chapels and churches and concert halls, from one end of the place to the other. It is a city infested with organs, and in this context I have a confession to make.

If it so happened, dear aged reader, that you were walking in Oxford one day in 1937, you may have been surprised to hear the strains of the 'Marseillaise' emerging fortissimo from St Aldate's Church, opposite Christ Church. The grand old anthem was being played on the organ over and over again, by no means impeccably, but *con spirito* and decidedly with all stops out. Why? you may have wondered – may perhaps be wondering still? Was it a national day in France, or some anniversary of the Entente Cordiale? Was some homesick expatriate furiously comforting himself ?

No, it was me, eleven years old and a pupil at Christ Church's college choir school close by. Somehow or other I had been let loose on that organ, and since the 'Marsellaise' was the only thing I could play on it, and I was everyone's patriot then as now, I made the most of the opportunity and sent that terrific anthem, blurred and approximate, time and again reverberating through the city.

Were you there in the street outside, that day in 1937? If so, *marchons, marchons*, and forgive me now!

DAY 144

A carnal little poem for my birthday (mostly fiction, by the way, but not entirely . . .):

You must eat up your salad
My mother used to say,
Like all such mothers everywhere,
From here to Mandalay,
From the beginning of the world,
Unceasing till today.

But now I am an adult, I care not what they say.
I am the lord of my cuisine, the captain of my tray!
In my house there's no salad. I've sent it all away.
No boring tasteless lettuce, no cucumber may stay.
Never a vegetarian now cares to come our way!

And if resistant mums still vainly hiss,
'There is no goodness in your carnal diet,'
I say, 'Dear Ladies, hold your prejudice!
Why not try it?'

Two happy things happened to me today. First, my eldest
son Mark, away in Alberta, told me that he is sending me
for my forthcoming birthday a first edition, dated 1871, of
E. W. Payne's *Glastonbury, or the Early British Christians*.
I have never heard of the work. Ms Payne was my great-
great-great-aunt, or something like that, and while I have
to say that our maternal literary forebears were seldom
sparkling performers, and wrote chiefly pious works for
children, still I shall be pleased and grateful to add her
book to the family shelf in our library, which contains, I
may add, a couple of books by Mark himself.

(He is keener than I am, by the way, on family trees,
forebears and such, but I must admit to being ridiculously
chuffed when he discovered some time ago that we are
directly descended on my mother's side from Hywel Dda,
the great Welsh law-maker (*c*.920–950). He was my grand-
father × 32! By now millions of Welsh people can probably
claim the same, but still . . .)

Anyway, the second nice thing that happened to me
today was the receipt, from dear friends in Charlottesville,
Virginia, of a photograph. They had taken it themselves,
they told me, during their walk home that afternoon, and
it showed a simple chalked graffito on a pavement. There
was the usual smiley face, and a heart, and a few childish
hieroglyphs; but largely near the edge of the pavement,

where nobody could miss it, were these magical words, boldly chalked:

BE KIND.

So all is not lost!

DAY 146

I have lived since kingdom come within sight of Snowdon, at 3,560 feet the highest mountain in Wales, and I think of it as a good old friend. It has never, however, actually excited me. It has size and presence, of course, but though it seems unkind to say it of such an acquaintance, to my mind Snowdon is short of charisma.

Down the years artists of great skill and fame have had their go at portraying its massif, but they don't seem to have been profoundly moved by it either. Of course, in the early days of mountain travel they loved to emphasize the thrilling awfulness of it all, those mighty ravines of legend, those dreadful chasms and inaccessible peaks, but I cannot help thinking they exaggerated their responses even then. And when truth crept in and more enlightened painters thought the area worth commemorating, somehow, in my view anyway, their innumerable canvases lacked magic.

How different seems to me a lesser mountain thirty miles or so to the south! Arenig Fawr is a far smaller peak, 2,800 feet high, but it has apparently had a much more mystic effect upon artists – and upon me. I have always found it movingly haunting, and in the 1930s a highly gifted group of post-impressionists felt its pull so power-fully that they went to live in its shadow and interpreted its presence in vivid canvases that briefly came to consti-tute a true school of art.

Many another artist has been drawn to Arenig since, and the reputation of the mountain was tragically climaxed, as it were, when in 1943 an American B-17 bomber, a 'Flying Fortress', crashed on its summit, killing all the crew. On a clear day I can just identify the silent peak of Arenig, away on our southern horizon, and my heart disloyally leaps; but there, honest old Snowdon understands.

DAY 147

I've been confused lately by the concept of 'wilding', the deliberate making of places wilder than they are by introducing species extinct or hitherto unknown in those parts. A much-publicized example of this human manipulation of nature was the reintroduction of wolves into the Yellowstone National Park in America. Eradicated by human intervention in the 1920s, they were brought back again in 1995 to deal with an overpopulation of elk by eating them. As an unexpected result, beavers proliferated, I can't quite remember why, and the whole food chain seems to have been affected by their newly ubiquitous dams, while the elks have proved themselves canny evaders of wolves after all.

So is everyone, animal or human, happy at Yellowstone now? I don't know, but the whole affair, and the whole conception of 'rewilding', makes me wonder what right the human race has to manipulate nature at all. Are we the bosses of the universe? Who says so? No doubt we are cleverer than any other creature, but does that give us the right to interfere with their very existence?

Our various human religions offer different answers, of course, but agnostic that I am, I have turned to the Bible, the Judaeo-Christian manual of morals, to find one for myself. There it boils down, essentially, to food (as it clearly did at Yellowstone). In the book of Genesis I learnt that God himself certainly decreed that we humans should be lords over all living creatures, down to every creeping thing that creepeth upon the earth, but close readings of the scripture suggest to me that we humans have no divine licence to eat any of it, but are divinely intended to be vegetarians.

One advantage of agnosticism, though, is that one can choose one's own rules, and this is my conclusion:

Treat all creation as equal, as you would wish all creation to treat you. Some creatures would like to make food of some of us, and some of us would like to make food of some of them. but as far as you can, temper it all with kindness, which is the supreme human conception, and which I suspect Nature knows little of.

I have a feeling that the British, deprived of their old confidence and self-satisfaction, may soon be nostalgic for their lost empire, for so long an epitome of political incorrectness. I hope they are. I have spent much of my life investigating and commemorating the old Raj, and long ago became convinced that although, of course, we now realize there was much that was deplorable in the very idea of imperialism – everyone knows that! – in its British interpretation there was much to be proud of too, and lots to be harmlessly pleased about.

The Empire certainly offered many perfectly decent British citizens enjoyable and worthwhile lives. At the top end of the scale were those whose careers quite plainly benefited everyone, rulers and ruled alike: doctors and nurses, engineers, scientists of many kinds, enlightened civil servants, teachers and geographers, and soldiers devoted to their men whatever their race, Geordies or Sikhs or Africans or Maoris. There were hundreds of thousands of such useful British imperialists, across a quarter of the world (and without question lots of them sometimes had doubts, as we do now, about the ultimate justice of their presence, however beneficial, among the palms and pines of Empire).

And then again, whatever the wrongs of imperialism, what harmless pleasure it could often be to a generation of

Britons, however misguided, who thought that presence morally OK! It seems to me that life in an imperial hill station, for example, must have been delightfully escapist: terrific landscapes, healthy climate, lively social life among friends, sports, Gilbert and Sullivan, Sunday service in the little Gothic church and hardly a whisper, I would guess, from one year to the next that the millions of friendly indigenes, all around, did not really want you to be there (for of course, then as now, political convictions did not necessarily clash with personal relationships).

Just a thought – but when the British, and particularly the English among them, ever get over their present condition of perpetual self-denigration, perhaps they will be able to look back at their imperial years with more pride to their apologies, and even, yes, a touch of nostalgia.

DAY 149

My eldest brother Gareth (1920–2007) was an eminent and scholarly professional flautist who was also, offstage as it were, a virtuoso *siffleur* – a whistler. He was particularly proud, he used to say, of his whistled performances of Paganini's *Perpetuum Mobile*, and he whistled all his life until his embouchure was damaged by a mugger in New York and he could whistle no more.

I am a whistler too, though not in a classical kind – I chiefly whistle to rhythmic purpose as I do my daily thousand-pace walk – and I am very much on the side of those people, now in a besmirched minority, who go about their lives with an often tuneless whistle, like errand boys of old. My heart is with them! As Disney's seven dwarfs told us long ago, 'When hearts are high / The time will fly / So whistle while you work!'

I was delighted, then, to learn the other day that another putative relative of mine was an accomplished whistler. Albert Payne, otherwise known as A. Ehrlich, was an Anglo-German music publisher in Leipzig at a time when my mother, Enid Payne, was a student at the conservatoire there. 'He played the violin very well,' I read in a contemporary memoir, 'but his real genius lay in whistling.' Herr Ehrlich could perform impossible things with his whistle, it seems, and it is reported that his performance of a Spohr violin concerto, with piano accompaniment, was just marvellous to hear.

I'm told that A. Ehrlich's classic book *Celebrated Violinists Past and Present* (1897) is still in print, but it's *Celebrated Whistlers Down the Centuries* that I would like to read, so perhaps I'd better write it.

On cats: I think of them a lot because I still miss my great friend Ibsen, the Norwegian Forest cat who died earlier in the year, and who must be the last of the long, long line of cats that have accompanied us all through our lives.

They have been animals of many kinds and breeds, and when the other day it seemed that Key West, at the southern tip of Florida, might be overwhelmed by a hurricane, I thought of Hemingway's house there, which is preserved as a museum together with descendants of his own large family of cats. I had been there, long ago, on a kind of pilgrimage. All those Hemingway animals were polydactyls – extra-toed cats – and at the time we had one, too, that I was very fond of. So I went to the house with sentimental purpose, because of all the cat kinds we have fostered down the years, Siamese and Abyssinians to plain dear moggies, Thug the big polydactyl was perhaps the nearest in my heart to Ibsen.

Well, I watched the news all last week and was relieved to find that Key West remained unscathed, and that the Hemingway House animals still thrived; and yesterday I saw on the TV some expert discussing the descent of the extra-toed cats that Hemingway had fostered over there. And do you know? The closest in origin to the polydactyl feline, he suggested, was the Norwegian Forest cat, which had big feet to cope with northern snows.

How marvellous! So Ibsen and Thug were cousins!

DAY 151

Day after day after day, although the world at large is in a condition of immense, portentous and hideously fascinating confusion, the morning news from London makes my heart sink with its tedium. The British nation is itself tottering on the brink of catastrophe, apparently unable to make up its mind about the abdication from Europe for which its electorate voted, in all ignorance, a year or two ago. It is enduring one of the most crucial challenges in all its long and magnificent history, threats to its very survival that could inspire, one might think, noble responses of oratory and debate.

You would not know it. For weeks not a single moving phrase has reached me over my breakfast table from the BBC. All is petty squabbling among the politicians, sprinkled with childish attempts at humour, and instinct only with personal and party ambition. What petty bores they nearly all seem to be, with only a handful of ageing backbenchers apparently trying to honour the grander traditions of their chamber! For the rest, dullards all, the whole lot of them, toffs and plebs alike. The news each morning from Trump's America is hardly more inspiring, hardly less saddening, but at least it often startles me with its effronteries. The news from Westminster, concerning the future existence of one of history's most fascinating constructions, just makes me yawn.

261

DAY 152

The news this morning tells me that the vast community of insects, all over the world, is on its way to extinction because of the insecticides, etc., that humans have used to improve their own condition. It will perhaps be the last stage, it is said, on the route to our own demise.

I am not surprised, used as I am to witnessing in my own garden, in my own minute patch of the globe, the gradual disappearance of fellow beings. The glow-worms have gone, and most of the dragonflies, and the lizards and the slow-worms and the grass snakes, the frogs and the toads and the hedgehogs and most of the caterpillars and many of the fish in our river. Like the steam train, they have gone the way of progress – human progress, that is. If I were God, I might be disappointed, I suppose, with the way things seem to be going, but perhaps I might think, Well, that's progress, that's those clever humans for you, winners are winners.

I would most certainly not approve, though, of the heedless manner in which, in small things as in big, our master species treats the lesser kinds en route to our common extermination. For example, if I decided to intervene, I would forbid the killing or chasing of any creatures purely for pleasure. I would stop local councils mowing the grass verges of roads, where insects live, just for tidiness. I would sneer at the pernickety artificialness of so many

262

gardens, which banish every last suggestion of wildness, including slugs. I would step in to control the miserable overbreeding of cats and dogs, creating so many freaks for prize money or profit. And, above all, I would abolish all those institutions, the world over, by which *Homo sapiens* sentences its less advanced colleagues to life for imprisonment, research, exhibition and entertainment purposes.

But then if I were God, I would say to Myself, contemplating such enormities, who have I made, what have I done? Shall I start again?

Today, my friends, I woke up despondent after a bad night, with thoughts about the miseries of nonagenarianism. A reader I met in the street yesterday had complained I'd got some dates wrong, and he had hit a nerve in me. What's the use of trying, I asked myself? Didn't the Bible say something about three score years and ten? Perhaps the euthanasians were right. It was a grey drizzly morning, that reader had depressed me, and I felt I had reached the age of pointlessness.

But lo! Look! The sun comes out, and after a quick breakfast I sit down at my desk to switch the computer on; and after exercising my fingers like a pianist, as I always do as a matter of form, I find myself settling down with all the old delight to the day's composition. What shall I write about today, dear friends? Good or bad, virile or senile, there's no life like the writer's life. Bugger that pedant! Love and laughs to everyone – JAN.

DAY 154

For the first time in my life I was taken up the mountain railway yesterday to the top of our neighbouring peak Snowdon, Yr Wyddfa, the highest in Wales or England. I enjoyed the experience immensely, but not in the way I expected. The line is closing for the winter, ours was the very last train on the timetable, and the whole venerable apparatus of the railway, which was built by Swiss engineers in 1864, was jam-packed with such a jostling, eager, multi-age, multi-race crowd, drawn here from the four corners of the earth, that I was irresistibly reminded of the Grand Trunk Road in India, as Kipling immortalized it in *Kim* – a river of life, 'all the world coming and going' . . .

The journey up was familiar enough to me, but still magnificent in its scale and landscape – and for my money more marvellous in its bare green grasslands than the snow wastes of your more famous Alpine funiculars. But whereas when I have wandered Yr Wyddfa alone I have felt myself to be in an empty world, whenever I looked out of the window from that train, somewhere down there, laboriously plodding up tracks, widely scattered across all flanks of the mountain, even scudding down it on bikes, were the thousands of other people who were with us on Snowdon that morning.

Then we reached the end of the line and tumbled out into a mist, and into a strange huge chamber which is actually a café but seemed to me that morning a kind of grand cauldron – a river of life indeed, not flowing exactly, but jammed higgledy-piggledy wherever there was space, a cheerful, amazed demonstration of humanity, eating sandwiches and rolls, with plastic cups of coffee, everyone talking at once, and laughing, and swapping encouragements or commiserations. And as I sat there myself, squeezed there with my own sausage roll, while some kind friend passed me a coffee over the heads of my neighbours, I had a sort of vision, rather as Kim did when he set eyes on that broad and smiling river . . .

For near the ceiling of the room, which itself remains something of a dream to me, there was a long window, and through it I could see dim, burly human figures clambering here and there in the mist. In fact, they were climbing the last few feet to the summit of Snowdon, to the cairn of stones at the very top, but they looked to me like initiates on some mystic mission, to achieve an ultimate destination before themselves fading into the fog.

So I felt a little mystic myself, as I started on the last of my sausage roll; but then a loudspeaker warned us that the final train was about to leave for the journey back to reality, so I gobbled it down, fast.

Patriotism is a problem, is it not? It can be so awful, but so noble too. I have been looking for patriotic music to illustrate a radio programme I'm working on, and the range of it is daunting, from boasting 'We've got the ships, we've got the men, we've got the money too' to building a new Jerusalem in England's green and pleasant land. The other day, though, searching American sources, I came across a recording by an elderly former marine of verse four of the US national anthem. He had thought it more Christianly proper than the usual first verse, I suppose because verse one seems to suggest that America's victories are purely secular, whereas verse four suggests that God Himself must preside over the triumphs of the Star-Spangled Banner.

As a Welsh agnostic, it was, of course, none of my business, but I rather agreed with this view, and I took to the old boy who presented it, so I popped my recording of his performance on to the Web and sent it to good liberal friends in America, hoping it might cheer them up at a time of national dejection. They acknowledged it, but notably without enthusiasm, probably because that venerable marine was performing at a meeting of a very right-wing political organization of which they understandably disapproved.

But dear me. When it comes to religion we simple free-thinkers can never win.

DAY 156

Today is a Sunday, and at a neighbouring village a chapel has been celebrating the 150 years of its existence – old age by Welsh Nonconformist standards. Of course, the congregation had a celebratory meeting this morning, and at lunchtime I came across an elderly acquaintance who had been there. 'Well,' said I, 'how did it go? Many people there?' 'Six,' she replied.

I am not a worshipper of any denomination, and by and large the chapel architecture of Wales is not to my taste, but nevertheless I am saddened always by the hundreds of abandoned chapels that litter our country – Calvinist Methodist, Methodist Calvinist, Independent Welsh Calvinist Methodist, and more obscure convictions that I know nothing of. A congregation of six must be a celebration – nil is the norm.

'Mind you,' my informant went on, 'I'm not really a chapel-goer myself. I'm an atheist.' She was old and very Welsh, and I did not believe her. 'I don't believe you,' I said, and she went on to tell me that she had not set foot in a chapel for years, until that very morning. 'I'm not at all sure that there is a God,' she said, and when I assured her that in that case she was not an atheist at all but an agnostic like me, she seemed rather relieved. She admitted that she enjoyed the music in Anglican churches, and had to agree that if there were half a dozen celebrants in her own

268

chapel that morning, most of our neighbours, whether Methodist or Anglican, Roman Catholic or even plain pagan, seemed to be as generally decent as they always had been.

So, obviously, was she. She had evidently gone to her chapel that morning convinced that she was some sort of hypocrite, but I am perfectly sure that Forgiveness, which in my book is a vital subsidiary of the Divine, was not in this instance required.

DAY 157

Right, this is the situation: it is the coldest day of the year, temperature minus 49 Fahrenheit, with a wind-chill factor of 830. The boiler has gone wrong, which means that we have no cooker or central heating, and none of the plumbers I have called are available. We are out of wood for our wood-burners, and anyway I can find no matches. The battery seems to be flat on my radio. Something has gone wrong with the television. It is starting to rain, and a stray cat is miaowing somewhere.

All this is more or less true, or feels like it, but when at last I get the news on the radio, and hear what is happening throughout the rest of the world, goodness me, what *am* I complaining about?

DAY 158

Here's a little private parable. Its text comes from a *New Yorker* cartoon by the late James Thurber concerning some not very good wine, a wine without breeding, as he called it – 'but I think you'll be amused by its presumption'.

Years ago, when I was young, I accompanied, as a reporter, the first expedition ever to climb Mount Everest. It made me a minor celebrity, and when a few years later the first flights to the moon were planned, it seemed to me that I was the obvious reporter to go with them – for I assumed, of course, that they would need one. Because of Everest I was well known for my experience in such adventurous projects, I had a high opinion of my own descriptive powers, and I only awaited the call.

Imagine the cheek of it! The sheer insolence! Think of how astronauts really are recruited, now that they go regularly into space – the infinite care with which they are chosen, the months of training and indoctrination, the scientific qualifications they need, the psychological requirements, the courage and dedication and technical skill, the sheer self-command of character!

The call never came, and a good thing too. I was by no means unassuming, unlike Thurber's wine, and looking back upon myself now, and marvelling at the calibre of the men and women who have since then been rocketed into space, I really cannot pardon my presumption.

Moral: Know Thyself, for Heaven's Sake.

For years, as I may have already told you, I have orchestrated my daily thousand-pace exercise to mental martial music of some kind – if not a stirring State anthem ('Deutschland, Deutschland über alles' or 'La Marseillaise'), at least some brisk piece of nationalist blarney like 'Waltzing Matilda', '(I'm a) Yankee Doodle Dandy' or a blaring wartime specimen of my youth called 'There'll Always Be an England'.

But I have lately made an extraordinary discovery: there is absolutely no category of music that cannot be marched to. No melody, however gentle or melancholy, cannot be adapted to the rhythmic tread of the parade. Try it! Try 'Your Tiny Hand Is Frozen', or 'Abide with Me', or a Brandenburg Concerto, or 'The Day Thou Gavest, Lord, Is Ended' – just fiddle around with the rhythm a bit and you will find that there is absolutely no category of music that is not adaptable to the sergeant-major's command!

This is a most welcome discovery for me, because to tell you the truth my repertoire of rousing marches was beginning to pall, and now my morning exercise is revivified. Only today I did my thousand paces to the music of a limpid Edwardian piece of sentimentality called 'I Passed by Your Window', and fine and fresh it was.

(Now I can't get the beat of it out of my head – 'I *passed* by your *win*dow, when *mor*ning was red, the *dew* on the *rose*bud, the *lark* overhead, and *Oh* I sang *soft*ly, though *no* one could *hear*, to *bid* you good *morn*ing, good *morn*ing, my dear!')

THAT'S IT! LEFT, RIGHT, LEFT, RIGHT, HEADS UP! EYES FRONT! GOOD MORNING, MY DEARS!!

As the United Kingdom seems to slither towards ignominy, and the lost British Empire is remembered chiefly
with shame, to my mind it is only the symbolic idea of
England that retains some sense of the grace, age and fascination of this ancient homeland. I don't count, of course,
the unfading allures of Wales and Scotland, I recognize the
arcane fascination of the crown, and for myself, a shameless romantic, I am also still susceptible to the grandeur
and bravado of imperial power; but what, I ask you, could
be less inspiring than the very name UK?

But 'England'! Even in its sad decline, there is to the
idea of England something wonderful, something graceful
and generous and green that is ethereally translated into
its name. Mimi in *La Bohème* catches it when she sings
of simple things that speak to her of love and spring, of
dreams and visions – 'things that are called poetry', and
perhaps it is indeed the poetry of Shakespeare's England,
subsumed through all its reputation, whose symbolic
influence down the centuries has been at the centre of the
English idea, and can still catch at the susceptible heart.

I suspect it reached the climax of its power during the
First World War, when a generation of English poets
spoke for the nation in its sorrows and reproaches. When
the Welshman Ivor Novello wrote one of the most popular
ballads of the time, he chose as a soldier's homesick war

aim the simple, the allegorical pleasure of walking with his lover 'down an English lane'.

An English lane, mark you, not a British lane, and it is that one word in the piece that still gives me a frisson today, a century on. When in 1958 Julie Andrews recorded a version in which an English lane became just a 'shady lane', all Mimi's gentle totemic magic left the song . . .

DAY 161

The Special Relationship is a once-familiar political phrase that is now moribund or discarded, but I believe in it still. Churchill first used it, I think, in the euphoric post-war years of victory, and he certainly exemplified it – his mother was American and his most ambitious work of scholarship was his *History of the English-Speaking Peoples*. And in my opinion that particular relationship still exists, like it or not, and still defines the particular affinity, instinctive, intellectual, that survives between the kingdom of Great Britain and its former colony, the United States of America.

You may scoff, whether you are American or British, and especially if you are young. You will probably tell me that America now lives in another sphere from Britain – the sphere of the contemporary great Powers, America and Russia and China and India, together with thrusting, modern newcomers around the world to whom Great Britain must seem almost pitifully passé.

But still, for the moment anyway, that particular link remains, and so like thousands of other Britons and Americans I represent in myself that Special Relationship. I have lived and worked in countries all over the world, but it is in America that I have made the most lasting friendships, shared the same moments of joy, pride or disillusionment. My very first book, sixty-odd years ago, was dedicated to the proposition that Americans were half-brothers of mine, and so I have felt it ever since. Come Roosevelt, come Trump, come a new world order, come the four corners in opinion against us, I shall always know, for what it's worth, that a few million Americans will be thinking just as I am, in special relationship . . .

DAY 162

Fame is the spur, Milton assured us, that elevates the
spirit, but in my opinion Shame is a more powerful
engine. I write with feeling, because I have just done
something I am ashamed of. For years my dear old Honda
Civic Type R, 2006 vintage, has been tended for me by
an obliging Scot, a famous rally navigator who owns a
garage along the road. The scrapes he has unscraped for
me, the dents he has undented, the wings he has replaced,
the engines he has rejuvenated, until by now the dear old
vehicle is far more than the sum of its parts, but a sort of
living resurrection of itself, feisty as ever and rejuvenat-
ing to drive!

Well, it went into Rob's garage last week for some attention to its innards, I forget what, and he lent me a very nice
courtesy car to use during its absence. Sentimentally, it
was not, of course, in the same class as my own old friend,
but as a matter of fact it was more powerful, much newer
and doubtless worth a great deal more money. Hardly had
I taken it over than I got it tangled up in scrubbery beside
our gate and tore the front end off it.

Shame knocked me askew and inflamed my spirit all
the more vividly when the dear man (stifling a curse, I
would guess) assured me I was forgiven . . .

DAY 163

A friend asked me yesterday to suggest a quotation that best expressed the spirit of our age, and before I had time to think offered me his own lovely but despondent choice, from Matthew Arnold's 'Dover Beach': 'And we are here as on a darkling plain . . . where ignorant armies clash by night.'

Well, I fear I agreed with him – ours is certainly an age of disillusionment, of abandoned faiths and hopes and even loves, and he is right, I'm sure, in believing that the sense of zeitgeist can best be expressed not in political, economic or even historic terms, but through the celestial medium of art. However, I'm damned if I'm going to let any old zeitgeist get me down, so I have searched through my jumbled poetic resources to find a proper retort, and stumbled upon these reminders that good humour, too, has its noble part to play in the passage of the ages:

> *Try I will; no harm in trying;*
> *Wonder 'tis how little mirth*
> *Keeps the bones of man from lying*
> *On the bed of earth.*

> *'Tis late to hearken, late to smile,*
> *But better late than never*

I shall have lived a little while
Before I die for ever.

From A. E. Housman, lad – who else?

I am not the only republican, I am sure, to feel some pleasure from the news that the man who is fifth in succession to the throne of Britain is to marry an American divorcée actress of mixed race who is three years older than he is and a dedicated feminist. For one thing, I have generally rather liked the sound of the ginger-haired Prince Harry, who really does seem a bit Shakespearean; and for another, well, of course I know nothing at all about Meghan Markle, never having heard of her before, but she looks all right and sounds interesting.

Naturally, though, much depends upon the royal wedding, which, as day follows night, will burst upon us in the spring, and which will either be as crassly ostentatious as its recent predecessors or may, by the example of Hal and Meg, conceivably persuade us cynics that family monarchy as a device of government is irrationally worth preserving.

DAY 165

My background music this morning, as I answered my mail, included one of Chopin's particularly exquisite preludes, which as usual tugged at my heart; and when my son Twm looked in I put to him a question that has often perturbed me: could a man who created such heavenly music be nasty? 'What about Wagner?' he instantly replied, and of course he had a point.

But only just. Hitler's maestro Wagner certainly gave us some profoundly beautiful melodies, but not in my view music instinct with the inspired simplicity and goodness that I long for, and which Chopin can provide.

On the other hand, was Chopin a good and simple man, any more than Wagner was, or should we never try to collate beauty with virtue? I don't know. Perhaps the truth is that Art is *sui generis*, beyond critical or intellectual judgement, and certainly beyond the crude values of the auction room or the pretensions of experts. 'I know what I like,' ordinary people say, to the scoffings of professionals, but I suspect their instincts, as against their opinions, are sometimes sounder.

I ornament my modest theme today, but why not? Bach often did.

DAY 166

I seem to remember that when I was a child, it was the practice to end a squabble with the incongruously classical cry, '*Pax!*' It seems to have worked, and I wish it did now. In a world of apparently endless and almost universal bickering, how refreshing it would be to be able to tell everybody, with a single imperative, just to shut up and leave us alone.

I felt the need especially when the mail came this morning, because it included a weekly magazine I subscribe to, and when with extreme difficulty I managed to tear its maddening packaging open, there fell out of it not just the publication itself, but, believe me, a positive welter of extraneous matter – advertisements, appeals, political propaganda, unwanted invitations, reminders about licences or debts, gushing suggestions concerning charities and even an instruction about how best to make my will.

'*Pax!*' I felt like crying. 'MYOB!' (as we also used to say) – 'Mind your own business!' But I have an unorthodox remedy for these moments of exasperation. Some sufferers, I know, rely upon Buddhist-style contemplation for their relief. I rely upon a ship. On one of our windowsills there stands a wooden model of an elderly paddle steamer which I brought home from Poland years ago. It flies the flag of the Free City of Danzig, which for forty years had its own constitution, national anthem, parliament,

284

government, postage stamps, currency and all – until on 1 September 1939 it was bombarded, invaded, seized and obliterated by the forces of Nazi Germany in the very first engagement of the Second World War.

You may well think such an aged souvenir of our times should be a reminder of aggressive interference, the awful spark that set the world alight; but no, for me it represents the opposite. There she lies in the sunlight, steamship *Leopold*, eighty years old but still fairly resplendent in her green, gold and faded crimson, with Neptune holding the trident of independence at her bows and the twin lions of the Free City on her paddle boxes. There is no stridency to her, no remorse either. She is emblematic of some of the very worst years in the history of the modern world, but she has sailed unflustered through it all, and so for me she represents, the dear old thing, the calm beyond the miseries, and a rebuff in my mind to all those damned meddlers . . .

DAY 167

I bumped into an acquaintance I admire during my morning walk today, walking briskly like me, and with the same intent. He is a retired physician, and he knows the physical, moral and intellectual value of exercise. This morning, however, he was not at his most invigorated, and I gathered it was because he did not quite know what was happening to people like him.

People like him? The sort of people, that is, who used to think of themselves as liberal-minded, free-thinking citizens of their society, and who now feel somehow exiled, trapped between prejudice and political incorrectness. As a doctor who had matured in the post-war society of Great Britain, I suppose his lodestar, as it were, had been the British National Health Service, a grand pioneering achievement of the time which exemplified what he was most proud of – generous, universal, high-minded public service, universally distributed. I asked him what he thought of the NHS now. He said it ought to be abolished, and I somehow had the sense that he had lost his way.

I suppose most of us these days, whatever our circumstances, wherever we live, are searching in some manner for a Way (*The* Way, gentle Buddhists say, but if we are to judge by recent events in Myanmar, even they seem to be losing it). I don't mean a political way, or an intellectual way, or even exactly a religious way, but something mistier and more nebulous, and there is an allusive kind of guide to it at the end of Kipling's strange masterpiece *Kim*. We seek the Road, the Lama tells his disciple Kim in its last pages, but we wondering readers never quite learn what the Road is, or where it will lead us. To the River of the Arrow? To the Justice of the Wheel? To the Presence of the Great Soul?

Wherever, the holy man concludes. The Search is ended anyway. He has wrenched his own soul back from the Threshold of Freedom and cries, to Kim as to us, 'Certain is our Deliverance!'

Got it, doc?

DAY 168

I can't help feeling sorry for those thousands of ageing gents, apparently half the world over, whose lives have been ruined by making improper suggestions, or touching women's private parts, or even reading sexy matter long, long years before.

I can remember the days when a playful pat of a lady's bottom was no more than friendly bonhomie. Reading smutty magazines under the bedclothes, whistling at susceptible passers-by or even making naughty suggestions were just adolescent goings-on, to be laughed at. Now a career can be ended, a reputation wrecked, if an elderly man is found to have indulged himself in this way in his youth. Of course, thank goodness, lots of odiously true sex pests and villains have been uncovered and properly punished, and in general sexual attitudes have become mercifully more civilized. But it seems to me that in many of the cases we read about the offence has been chiefly against good taste.

The offenders evidently were, if not actually villainous, not very *gentlemanly* youths, and could it perhaps be that they are now, however innocent and distinguished, not very fastidious elders? Are we being governed and dazzled by elderly vulgarians, however distinguished? Or can we generally assume that such politicians and celebrities have, as parents used to say in those olden times, 'grown out of it'?

I do hope so. 'Say you're sorry,' the parental watchword used to be, and I hope it was usually enough.

Advent Sunday, and it began magnificently when I got out of bed and turned on the BBC to hear their morning Christian service from some English cathedral or other. The agnostic liberty allows me to take my satisfactions, like my doubts, from any source of faith, and I love the old Anglican choral traditions and the antique words of the Authorized Version of the Bible.

Well, as I say, it started splendidly, with a fine choir and an apparently enthusiastic congregation singing one of Charles Wesley's magnificent hymns, joyous and thunderous. 'Wonderful,' I said to myself as I conducted it in my pyjamas, 'sometimes they really do get things right!' As they sang to the last long chord of the hymn, fortissimo, I imagined to myself the black-cassocked preacher opening an antique prayer book, behind the gilded eagle of his lectern, for the first prayer of the morning; and sure enough, when the music faded, there sounded the opening words of the supreme Christian prayer:

'Our Father, who are in Heaven . . .'

'*WHICH ART* IN HEAVEN . . .' I screamed, as I slammed the radio off and got back into bed for a further snooze after all. Dear God, they were using that dreadful modern translation of the divine appeal, instead of the majestic King James translation of 1611. There and then

I apologized to the Almighty on their behalf, crossing my
fingers pedantically.

Thinking again about The Way, that nebulous religio-philosophic-poetic-politic-mystical conception of fulfilment, I watched on TV one of David Attenborough's virtuoso programmes about the seas, and marvelled at the skills, imagination and sheer chutzpah of the project. Miles beneath the surface of some tropical ocean a team of human scientists and cameramen crawled about in their vehicle in the darkness, reliant for their survival entirely upon their own instruments, mechanisms, knowledge, skills and courage. And all around them, on my screen that evening, extended a vast dark wilderness, as far as my eye could see, inhabited by millions and millions of strange creatures, all busily pursuing their own ends in an apparently endless pitch-dark cavern.

Did those swarming sub-aquatic creatures conceive some ethereal Way of their own fulfilment, their own Destination? I really cannot think so, and I am tempted to conclude today, as I watch that sunless, heaving mass of beings, that Attenborough's revelatory projects really only confirm Macbeth's verdict: the whole vast phenom-enon of life itself, human to fish, skylark to hippopotamus to sea slug, really signifies nothing in particular, however fascinating the TV . . .

DAY 171

I am pleased to see that this year's Stirling Prize for architecture has gone to the reconstructed pier at Hastings in East Sussex, because I have a weakness for British pleasure piers and all that they long represented in the character of the nation. I spent part of my childhood in the company, as it were, of a famous example: the pier built in 1869 at Clevedon, on the north Somerset coast of the Bristol Channel, looking across to Wales. It was built essentially as a sort of extension to the burgeoning railways, providing a connecting steamship service to the Welsh ports, but it presently became a place of pleasure too. It was there, when I was perhaps five years old, that I was introduced to my very first members of the theatrical profession, from a concert party performing a season at the pier; and it was from that same venerable jetty that my mother used to take the White Funnel lines paddle steamer to Cardiff to broadcast her piano recitals.

Those are decorous memories, though, from a decorous little place (John Betjeman loved Clevedon Pier, which flourishes still), but anything but decorous is the aura that to this day attends the general reputation of the British seaside pier. On the contrary, the memory is bawdy, bold, a little risqué, frankly vulgar and fun. It goes with not very naughty picture postcards that have become a collectors' genre of their own, often featuring a fat jolly holiday-maker looking through a slot machine to see What the Butler Saw. There are still scores of pleasure piers around the British coasts, but their heyday ended when so many of the British of all classes threw themselves into foreign tourism and began spending their summer holidays at places like Biarritz or Benidorm instead of places like Blackpool.

I miss the seaside crowds of the old days, the days of my innocent youth, when they seemed to me like a nation of their own. How fundamentally decent they all appeared to be, how agreeable, how proud and fond of their families. They and their dads and mums had been through wars, depressions, strikes, deprivations and disillusionments. Yet I still think of them in my mind, in the abstract as it were, as part of a grand, cheerful and wholesome unity.

Of course, I am talking nonsense. But there we are – that's What the Butler Showed to me!

DAY 172

My heart bleeds today for the Royal Navy.

An anecdote I cherish from the Second World War concerns the simultaneous arrival at some port or other of two warships, one from the US Navy, one from the RN. 'Good morning!' the cheerful American commander is supposed to have signalled. 'How's the world's second-biggest navy this morning?' 'Fine, thanks,' replies the British ship. 'How's the second-best?'

Only a friendly joke, but it rang pathetic when it came into my mind this morning, because the news contained yet another ignominy for the British navy. Not only, of course, is it now infinitely smaller than the gigantic American fleet, but it would be a crazed patriot indeed who would claim it to be better.

So much seems to have gone wrong with it lately – collisions, breakdowns, over-costings, errors. As an awful example take the Type 45 destroyers, trumpeted in the 1960s as the new backbone of the fleet. First there were going to be twelve of them, then eight, and finally only six put to sea, three years late and vastly over cost. Never mind, said the First Sea Lord, they were the Navy's most capable destroyers ever ... Unfortunately, their engines and propellers kept going wrong and they so overheated that they could not be used in hot climates, so that they have spent most of their time in port, sometimes all six at the same time.

And then this morning I heard on the news that the aircraft carrier *Queen Elizabeth*, brand-new flagship of the British fleet, had sprung a leak. Sprung a leak! She is the biggest and most expensive vessel ever built for the Royal Navy, the third to carry the name, and she was accepted into service only the other day by the Queen of England in a vastly ostentatious dockside ceremony. At 70,000 tons and a cost of several billion pounds, perhaps she deserved hyperbole, and I suspect the leak was not really as comical as it sounds, but I fear all the same that she may really represent a sad last hurrah of an ancient and magnificent tradition, one that I have always cherished.

Yesterday I piled up some bags of logs on the floor of our library, to be taken upstairs today for our wood-burning stove, and when I started on the job just now I happened to notice that the bags totally obscured a row of books in one bookcase. Guess what they were? Right first time. *A History of the Royal Navy* in seven proud and splendid volumes.

Sprung a leak? Laugh? I could have cried.

One morning in 1956, when my family and I lived on our houseboat *Saphir*, on the Nile, in Cairo, the mail turned up as we were having breakfast on the deck with a visiting guest. It included a package from London, and when I opened it, with rising excitement, I found it to contain the very, very first copy of my very, very first book, *Coast to Coast* (Faber and Faber, 271pp, 21s.). Our guest watched my pleasure as I unwrapped it, and then laughingly said, 'As long as you live, you'll never have another moment quite like this!'

Well, she was wrong. This morning, half a century on, when we sat at our luncheon table in Wales there arrived in the mail my very first copy of my very latest book, *Battleship Yamato* (Pallas Athene, 112pp, £9.79). I have published forty-odd books by now, a couple are on the stocks and Fabers are waiting to publish another posthumously, but the unwrapping of *Yamato* has excited me just as much today as did the arrival of *Coast to Coast* all those years ago, and so has every single one of those books since then!

If our guest of the *Saphir* happens to read this, I hope she is amused; but like the houseboat itself, she long ago sank, and must be laughing, dear soul, somewhere else . . .

DAY 174

In memoriam: the Aardvark and five Meerkat brothers who died in a fire during their unforgivable captivity at the London Zoo, 23 December 2017.

DAY 175

Christmas 2017 has come and gone, and Scrooge with it. I must admit that during the last few days I have all too often felt him a comrade. *'Bah!'* I have growled to myself when yet another Christmas Special has appeared in my TV screen, or yet another greetings card has turned out to be grossly commercial, or scrawled by some infinitely remote acquaintance whose signature I cannot read and who provides no return address. My conscience has been provoked by the thought that I have been too stingy with my presents to grandchildren, nephews and nieces. *'Humbug!'* I have sworn when those damned Jingle Bells rang yet again through the drizzly day of celebration.

But Boxing Day dawned glorious, and when I went down to our beach I found the whole world in generous festivity, children dashing about on modernistic roller skates, indulgent dads throwing stones into the sea for the entertainment of their dogs, mothers laughingly gossiping, people I hardly knew asking after the family, people I did not know at all just saying hullo, balloons blowing about and the odd brave jogger determinedly jogging anyway.

At the end of the beach I came across an Indian, all alone, standing above the pebbles gazing out to sea. There was nothing to be seen out there, only mist and distant hills, but when I wished him good morning he just smiled gently, and looking out across the waves again, quietly murmured, 'Glorious.'

'*God bless us every one*,' cried Tiny Tim happily, and I went on my way humming.

DAY 176

Here, on the last day of 2017, is my personal portent for the future.

Puzzled by the use in the media of the word 'millennials', for the first time in my life I turned to artificial intelligence to tell me what it meant. Speaking into my computer I asked Siri, the cybernetic information service, what millennials were, and in a trice some gentlemanly mechanism explained that they were people born between the early 1980s and the early 2000s. I needed no dictionary or encyclopedia. Instantly, in a flash, artificial intelligence had given me my answer, and given me my portent too.

I have no doubt that all the immense heavings and stirrings in the world today, the challenges and the triumphs, the anxieties, the tragedies, the visionary movements, the risings and fallings of nations and the hopes of ideologies – all are insignificant beside the gigantic prospects of artificial intelligence. Already we have cars that can drive themselves, robots that can outplay chess grandmasters or engage humans in sensible conversation, and within the next few years robots will be putting hundreds of thousands of people out of jobs and throwing the world economy out of kilter.

We, the humans, have achieved all this, and I have no doubt that before long we shall have succeeded in giving our robot surrogates feelings too, and creative faculties, and a full range of emotions, until in the end they achieve autonomy and can do without us.

And then what? We shall have succeeded in creating ourselves, and for me that fateful crescendo began when Siri told me this morning what millennials are, and I said 'Thank you.'

DAY 177

In memoriam: the thirteen monkeys who died in a fire at the monkey house of the Woburn Safari Park in Bedfordshire, unforgivably far from their homeland, on 2 January 2018.

DAY 178

The News from America

I woke up today with a challenging bump.
Whom do I trust? Is it Bannon or Trump?
Who is this Wolff, who has written that book?
Tillerson, Kushner – are they worth a look?

Should I stick with The Times, *for reliable views,*
Or is Twitter the place to keep up with the news?
'And where's Uncle Sam?' half-awake I inquire –
'Why on earth is he floundering there in the mire?'

I had no reply, so went back to my sleep.
To hell with it all – it will keep, it will keep.

The News from London

I got up this morning and heard something sinister:
Plotters had plots to remove our prime minister!
Some were against her because of her Brexit,
Others (bad rhymers) called her dyslexic.
They claimed that our nation could never be great
If she was commanding the Ship of the State,
And said that her running of the economy
Might well have come straight out of old Deuteronomy.
(From the Bible, they meant – as much as to say
That all was too much for poor Mrs May!)

And to tell you the truth I am not at all sure
Which opinion is phony,
Which judgement is pure . . .
So over my breakfast I'd rather recall
When we thought our poor country the greatest of all.
And then I shall sing, while my coffee's still hot
Britain, Britannia, best of the lot!

DAY 180

Since the start of 2018, in our particular corner of Wales, we have been seeing rainbows – such rainbows! Vivid rainbows, shimmering rainbows, rainbows dominant, rainbows gentle and apparently permanent – until, of course, as all things magic do, they falter and fade and disappear.

I have never seen such rainbows before, and several times, when I have glimpsed one through my window, I have jumped into my car and gone in search of it – and do you know, honestly, I have very, *very* nearly reached the patch of glimmering glory where the rainbow ends and the pot of gold lies – quite close sometimes, just at the end of the lane, just over the river, just behind the Parrys' farmyard – until, ah, just before I reach it, it is never there after all . . .

But believe me, when the rainbow deigns to visit our corner of Wales and displays itself in full resplendence against our background of bare mountain and empty sea, no Beethoven or Turner, no Shakespeare or Grecian architect could outshine its inspiration. Just now, as I thought about this little paean, it occurred to me to play my recording of Judy Garland singing Harold Arlen's 'Over the Rainbow' in 1939, and the tears have come into my eyes.

DAY 181

Self-pity is seldom attractive, and lately I have been feeling shamefully sorry for myself. The other day I pulled out of a broadcast I was going to do for the BBC, simply because I did not feel up to it – as I feebly excused myself. I told them that old age, shaky health, fading powers and personal anxieties had persuaded me that it was time to opt out, and they were very nice about it and said they quite understood.

What a miserable surrender that was, and I pulled out of several other commitments too, and declined some new engagements, and in general behaved as though I was about to retire from public view. And today? Well, today I half regret it, but only half. I was right in some of my assessments, alas, but wrong in others.

Poor me, on a cusp – between vigour and exhaustion, between pride and regret, between life and . . . Well, after all, I am in my ninety-second year . . .

Oh, do shut up. Talk about maudlin! See you next time.

DAY 182

On my recent birthday my beloved son Twm and *his* love Gwyneth wrote for me a celebratory song entitled 'Kindness and Marmalade', recognizing that those two commodities have played crucial parts in my life.

You may laugh, but it is true. As to kindness, well, I have been boring people till kingdom come with my conviction that it is the ultimate virtue, embracing all others, understood by everyone, recognized by most religions and a pleasure to practise.

A devotion to marmalade is perhaps less comprehensible, but for many years I have been an addict of that cult too. During half a lifetime of travel, I took a pot of marmalade wherever I went, in war as in peace, in pleasure as in frenzy. In 1953, I took a jar of Cooper's Oxford to assist my reportage of the first ascent of Mount Everest, and at a hundred foreign breakfasts I have preferred my own condiments to theirs.

Now that I am mostly at home in Wales, as Twm and Gwyneth recognized, I have not neglected the old loyalty. By now, I admit, there is an element of superstition to my marmaladia. Seven jars are aligned on our kitchen dresser, one for each day of the week, and each is different – all brewed, if that's the verb, in Wales, some home-made by friends, some just from Welsh companies, but each one individual in taste as in association.

I eat from them in strict order, Monday to Sunday, and just occasionally I get the day wrong, and my toast gets marmalade from Ty Newydd, say, when it should be from Caffi'r Tyddyn, or vice versa. This is a black discovery for me, and I expect a day of bad luck to follow. Then again, I admit to moments of faithlessness in occasionally enjoying barbarisms like lemon or even whisky flavourings in my marmalades.

Such heresies must expect retaliation, unless I expiate them by sincere apologies to the marmagods. But they are sure to forgive me anyway. Their congregations are none too large, and they can hardly afford to be vindictive . . .

DAY 183

The news that on British Airways first-class passengers are no longer to have flowers on their tables strikes me poignantly, and reminds me of the happy days I spent, in the 1950s and 1960s, wandering the world in airliners at other people's expense. It is true that the publishers and magazine editors who were my benefactors generally sent me by business or club class, but in those days they were sufficiently pretentious anyway, and for the most part I travelled lordlily (yes, there is such a word – I've just looked it up).

For example, I see from my package of old mementos that when one day I flew by Pan Am to Hong Kong, the luncheon menu offered me not merely a Filet Mignon, but sautéed eggplant and Diet Coke too, while United Airline's Tasteful Sampling included Breast of Duck enhanced by Chives and Lingonberry. When Virgin Atlantic once flew me to New York, I lunched upon a Medley of Steamed Lobster and Halibut, with a Sacher Torte to follow, and I shall never forget afternoon tea with British Airways on my way to Miami – a croissant filled with smoked turkey and tuna fish, garnished with radish, egg and mustard-flavour filling, and followed by fruit cake with peanut cookie and chocolate.

You see? We knew how to fly in those days, did we not?! I can laugh at the pretensions now, but I look back at it all with affection. Who could resist a tot of United Airline's Royal Lochnagar whisky, coming as it did from 'a tiny distillery no more than a stone's throw from the royal castle at Balmoral'? And who could fail to hang on to the delightful little keepsakes that came with the cuisine if we were crossing the Atlantic on the ultimate airliner, British Airways' Concorde – the most beautiful and, alas, one of the least successful flying machines ever built?

I have two of them before me now, both proudly marked with the Concorde emblem. One is a beautifully packed set of playing cards, the other an exquisite little monogrammed notebook. I have never used the playing cards nor written a single word in the notebook.

DAY 184

About Inventions

When I was a cadet at Sandhurst in the closing phase of the Second World War, I invented a device which was something to do with gunnery in tanks in action. I forget exactly what it was, but it was awfully clever. It concerned, I think, communications between a tank commander, viewing the battle scene with his head stuck out of the turret, and the gunner below him inside the tank. However, nobody seemed impressed by the device, whatever it was, and so it became the first of my unsuccessful inventions.

The second also concerned tank warfare. This was a way of making absolutely certain that the open iron hatch of a tank did not close with a bang when it went over a bump, and its failure was vividly demonstrated to me when the hatch of the Sherman tank I was commanding on some exercise shut so violently upon my left hand that I can still see the distortion of my fingers, seventy years on.

More ambitiously in my inventing career, it seemed to me that when mankind first defied space and sent rockets here and there in the universe, a homely opportunity was wasted. In one of my spasms of brilliance it occurred to me that if the world really was round, as was generally thought in those days, and was constantly rotating, one could send a passenger rocket up into space, pause it while the revolving earth reached the desired spot below, and then land it and its passengers safely in Timbuktu, Newfoundland or Heathrow.

This idea was greeted with uniform derision, but here is one last invention which seems to me at once practical and desirable. When I drive from my house into Cricieth, our nearest town, I reach a three-way junction. I can turn right or left, or go straight over. My indicator, of course, will flicker left or right, but it has no way of warning pedestrians or traffic that I am going straight ahead.

I suggest having a three-way indicator, so to speak, in every car. I have touted this invention around for half a century, without response, so if somebody at Honda. co.uk reads this, here is a message direct from my friend and companion Honda Civic Type R, 2006 vintage, age 106,000 miles:

PLEASE SAVE ME FROM IGNOMINY IN MY OLD AGE BY FITTING ME WITH A THREE-WAY TRAFFIC INDICATOR, AS ADVOCATED BY J. MORRIS.

LOVE AND THANKS IN ADVANCE FROM L432 WJC

I don't know about you, but recent events suggest to me that we stand upon one of the final cusps of human history, when everything we know is on the brink of change. The instincts of zeitgeist, the rivalries of States or cultures, the squabbles of politicians, the squalid ambitions of capitalists and even the compensations of religion seem to me almost comical considered in the perspective of our times.

Great God! On one level we are seeing the entire balance of political power shifting day by day, as proud old nations give way to brilliantly ambitious newcomers, armed with new ideas and ambitions and revolutionary weapons. Don't the tank, the battleship, the submarine and even the bomb already begin to feel obsolete, challenged by the cyber-armoury? Couldn't a rocket from one State destroy the capital of another with the mere touch of a button? The loftiest Powers of our time are humiliated already, deprived of their certainties, and the Trumps and Putins of our day already seem out of date.

And looming over everything, in my view, is the gigantic advance of artificial intelligence. I read today that in China they have cloned a couple of macaque monkeys, pictured, poor little souls, looking like wan and bewildered orphans. Be not afraid, Zhong Zhong and Hua Hua, you will not be alone for long. And if man can create a monkey, soon he will be able to create himself – or if he won't, no doubt some created monkey will!

Good morning, all. It's a pleasant day in Wales.

DAY 186

When the skies are clear, once or twice a day I see the silent white streaks of vapour trails high among the clouds, and they never fail to move me. They always seem to travel in couples, one after the other like pairs of faithful friends, and they are always flying purposefully to the west. I assume they are airliners from England, or perhaps from the continent of Europe, on their way to America, but it is the silent enigma of their passage that fascinates me.

I get the same sense of mystery from birds. Day after day I wonder, as I watch the birds in our garden, or down by the seashore, what on earth they are all up to, and what enables or obliges them to do whatever it is they are doing. Today, for instance, a small flock of terns flew over my head and settled on the sea's surface a few hundred yards out. I watched them attentively through my binoculars, and what do you think they *were* doing? They were doing absolutely nothing at all. They simply sat there, gently bobbing up and down with the tide. They were not eating anything, or foraging, or even apparently communicating with each other. They simply sat there on the sea, until quite suddenly, for no apparent reason, they rose from the water as one and flew back over my head into the fields behind.

What were their purposes? Were they preparing for some immense migratory flight later in the year? Were they obeying some celestial instructions? Whatever their intentions or obligations, I saw them as remote ancillaries of those high white vapour trails, silently, silently navigating the empyrean . . .

Today, a review of a book of beautiful aerial photographs
of Wales:

> *In Miami the sunshine is better,*
> *In Venice hyperbole fails.*
> *There's probably nowhere much wetter*
> *Than perpetually waterlogged Wales.*
>
> *But the old place can seem quite marvellously fair*
> *From viewpoints sufficiently high in the air . . .*
>
> *Bless its heart. That's art!*

DAY 188

A Day in Old Age!

Here's how it went:

I decided yesterday that I would have my dear old car professionally washed and cleaned (for the first time, as it happens, during the long happy years of our association – I prefer a well-worn Honda).

I would spend the rest of the day knocking off various humdrum duties too. So after breakfast I drove along the coast to our nearest town with my dear Elizabeth – who is, as the saying goes, beginning to show her age, and likes a ride.

First we went to the offices of my accountants, where I left a grubby envelope of bills, receipts and such, enabling them, I hope, to estimate my taxable income to the Inland Revenue for the year before last (I think). They wanly accepted it, and Elizabeth and I drove on to the public waste dump dutifully to relieve ourselves of a vast black bag of miscellaneous rubbish. Much of this Elizabeth would not consider rubbish at all, so I handed it over to the foreman, an old friend of mine, without letting her see, before moving hastily on to our second-nearest town, where we proposed to get the car done. I dropped it off with some agreeable Poles who run a car-washing business, and they told us to be back in an hour.

We then walked the half-mile or so to a pleasant restaurant we know to have some lunch. It was closed. So we walked another mile or so to another coffee shop for a snack instead. While we were there I discovered my credit card was missing, so we hurried back to the car washers to see if I had left it there. I hadn't, so we walked another five miles or so across town to the local branch of my bank to get some cash to pay the car washers with, and then retraced our steps back to the closed restaurant in case I had dropped the card on the way.

I hadn't, so we walked back the ten miles to the coffee shop, and while I emptied my bag and wallet in a last search for the card, my beloved Elizabeth looked in *her* bag and found it had been there all the time. We walked in sultry silence the twenty-five miles back to the car-wash place, where the Poles were very welcoming and gave me back my car.

It looked unnaturally new, but never mind, it will soon look itself again – we must all recognize our ages, must we not? Anyway, it went very well on the drive home, and we ended the day delightfully with mussels and white wine by the sea.

And so to bed.